The Beginner's Guide to C++
James Kelley

The Beginner's Guide to C++
James Kelley
© 2014

Author's Web Site: www.gurus4pcs.com

If you find an error, have a question or have something to add to this publication, email me at jkelley742@gmail.com.

Dedications:
>   My son Mike who field tested this book in his High School class.
>   My wife Joan who put up with my many hours at the keyboard writing this text.

Preface

This course was designed to work with Microsoft Visual C++, Microsoft Visual C++ Express and DevC++ a free download C++ compiler. Note that there are examples that show the use of all the statements covered in the text. Enter this code, make it work, understand what each statement does and when a particular statement is used.

There are 32 lessons in this tutorial. If you are a complete beginner start with lesson 1 and proceed through each lesson in sequence. If you just need to refresh on a certain topic, there is a table of contents that you can search for the lesson that contains the material you need.

The way to learn a programming language is by doing. Do the sample code, use the code to create your own programs. Go on the internet and find other programs and modify them to do another task or change the way they do the task they were assigned to do. Use what you are learning and you will master C++. Remember, no one learned to ride their two-wheel bike by just reading about how to ride. At some point you have to get up there and take some bumps. Just like riding the bike, you are not a good confident rider until you have practiced riding over and over, you will not be a good programmer until you have written many programs. You will be successful if you apply the same persistence as you applied to riding a two-wheel bike to learning how to write C++ programs.

This course was designed to be conducted using smaller segments of instruction. The emphasis is on the "hands-on" portions of the class.

If you would like the test bank, source code for the examples and the lab exercises I use, please email me and all I ask is: (1) how you are using the book (class, personal, reference, etc.); (2) where you live; (3) your comments on the book (likes, dislikes, need to add, etc.). My email address is: jkelley742@gmail.com.

Table of Contents

SECTION I - Using C++

CHAPTER 1
Overview of C++

Objectives:
- Identify various C++ compilers
- Describe Microsoft's Visual C++
- List the steps to compile an executable file
- Explain the programming process.
- Describe the statements common to most C++ programs.

Lesson 1.1 USING VISUAL C++

The Microsoft Visual Studio Programming Suite contains Visual C++, Microsoft's implementation of the C++ programming language. The Microsoft C++ IDE (Integrated Development Environment) provides several tools to make programming in C++ much easier. First there is the Editor which helps you format your program and color codes various segments of your program. Next, the ability to compile and debug your programs, point and click. Should there be errors in the way you have written your code statements (*syntax errors)* in your program, the IDE will try to point you to the approximate line number where the error was detected (Note the word approximate). Appendix A will explain how to build your first C++ program.

Lesson 1.2 Why learn C++?

The C++ language is one of the most widely used programming languages in the industry. It is extremely flexible in its ability to solve problems from basic business applications to complex scientific applications. This wide range of application make it a popular language in education, scientific, engineering, and the business world. You can find the current ranking of C++ as a programming language choice by going to the web site www.tiobe.com.

Lesson 1.3 Where is the C++ language used?

The C++ programming language can be used to develop a wide range of applications. It can be used by any local business to write a program to do their payroll or solve some other business problem requiring a custom built solution. It may be used by a software developer to create a commercial package for a common application like a word processor or an accounts receivable package. It is also used in Government, Military, aerospace and the scientific community. Most engineering majors are required to take a course in C++ programming as it is widely used in engineering applications.

C++ is a compiled language, so it is used where speed of processing is important. Compiled means that the program contains all of the commands required by the program in the ones and zeros that the computer needs to do its processing.

Lesson 1.4 Different C++ Compilers

Microsoft Visual Studio (Visual C++) is a commercial product that is part of the Visual Studio.NET suite of development software. It comes with an excellent editor, compiler, debugger and runtime environment. Microsoft offers an Express version which is a free download from their Dreamspark web site for Express software.

DevC++ is a free C++ compiler available from http://www.bloodshed.net, Bloodshed Software and you can download it to your PC. It is an Open Source offering so it is the full version that will not expire or will you ever be asked to make any purchase. There is limited support available on the internet.

gcc Compiler The gcc compiler is included in almost every Linux Operating System implementation. C++ is widely used in the Linux community for software development. Many of the applications available for the Linux operating system were written in C++ and some downloaded software will require compilation before they can be used.

Lesson1.5 Compiling a Program

Create Source Code
Enter the code required to solve the problem. This is a plain text file that consists of the C++ framework containing C++ commands. These commands are stored in a file with a .cpp extension.

Compile the Code
The compiler turns the source code into the ones and zeros that the computer understands. This is then written to a file with an .obj extension

Link in the Libraries
Some commands we use in C++ require additional code to complete their function. This code is stored in files called libraries. This is tested code that you benefit from because it can greatly reduce the number of commands you need to write by using pre-written and tested code. The result of this process is a file with a .exe extension.

Executable
Once you have an executable file it can then be transported to any other PC with a suitable operating system and run, just as well as it did on the computer that created it. Note that programs created by Visual C++ will require that the computer running the executable has the current .NET framework installed.

Finding Files
When you have everything working you may want to find the source and executable files. By default, Microsoft puts a project folder in the Project folder within the Visual Studio folder found in the user's document folder. There are several sub folders in the project folder and depending on the version, the .cpp (source) and .exe (executable) will be found in one of these folders.

Lesson 1.6 The Programming Process

Understand the Problem
Before the programmer can do anything they must have a solid understanding of the problem to be solved by the computer program they are about to create.

Analysis
The programmer must break the problem down into the logical steps and algorithms required to solve the problem. This is generally accomplished with flowcharts, pseudocode, IPO charts and other analysis tools.

Code
This is the step where the programmer writes the source code to solve the application problem. When coding is complete, the programmer compiles the program, fixes any errors and repeats the process until the compiler can produce an executable file.

Test
Now that we have an executable file the programmer must make sure the program produces accurate and consistent results. There should be a set of test data that tests all possible conditions the program may encounter in the course of normal (or even abnormal) operating conditions.

Implementation
Once the program is free of errors and has been proven to produce accurate and consistent results, it can be put into production. Users trained to operate the program, documentation written to explain how the program works and what it does, and placed on the computers or servers that will host the application program.

Maintenance
Even after a program is in use, the users will find problems like, errors in calculation and often add new things the program should do that were never thought of before. This is the maintenance phase and is ongoing throughout the life of the program. Even such well known application programs like Windows, Word, Excel, etc. all have periodic updates done to fix problems found.

Lesson 1.7 Programming Style

Exercising care in how you lay out your programs is an important step in making your programs easy to read and maintain. As we introduce various elements of C++, we will demonstrate a particular style of programming. When you develop a style of programming it should be used consistently. Some of the elements of good programming are good use of comments, proper indentation, consistent naming styles for variables and constants and proper attention to case (uppercase and lowercase letters).

Proper use of comments means that you put comment lines before your program that identify the name of the source file, the author, the date of the program and the purpose of the program. You also place comments at key places in the code to explain what a particular section of code has been designed to do.

Proper indentation means that you indent lines of code consistently to add readability to your code. There is nothing harder to follow than a program that does not use indentation consistently. Indentation helps you track where a section of code starts and ends. This is a big help when you are trying to determine where a statement block starts and ends.

Consistent naming styles for variables and constants. One style for constants is to make them in ALL UPPERCASE. Then when you are looking at code you know that when you encounter a variable name in all uppercase it is a constant. Naming your variables should be done in one of three ways, pick one and stick with it. (1) all lowercase characters; (2) Camel case starting with a lowercase letter and using uppercase to separate words, for example, payrate would be written payRate. (3) Using underscores in place of spaces to separate words like payrate would be written pay_rate. We will discuss this later when we cover variables and constants.

Most C++ programmers stick with lowercase whenever possible. Many programming languages are case sensitive and a programmer is always safe in using lowercase exclusively. C++ variable names are case sensitive, so when writing variable names you need to write them the same way in the code as you declared them initially. Short meaningful names using one of the three styles we mentioned earlier are the best way to avoid the dreaded "variable name not declared" error message.

```cpp
// programname.cpp
// Date:
// Author:
// This program demonstrates good style and comments
#include <iostream>
using namespace std;

int main()
{
  // declare variables
        int num1;
        int num2;
        int answer;
  // get data from users
        cout << "Enter a Number";
```

```
        cin >> num1;
        cout << "Enter a Number";
        cin >> num2;
    // processing here
        if (num1 < num2)              // determine if num2 is larger than num1
            answer = num2 - num1;     // if true subtract num1 from num2
        else                          // if it is false
            answer = num1 - num2;     // subtract num2 from num1
    // display results
        cout << "The answer is: " << answer << endl;
    return 0;
}  // end of main function
```

Lesson 1.8 C++ TEMPLATE

All C++ program exercises and examples in this book will use the same basic template. There is
a group of statements common to all C++ programs we will be working with.

A skeleton C++ program is shown below. This is the minimum code for all of your C++
programs. Putting the comments up front (all the lines that begin with //) is important to
identifying your program. I have also listed names for the files you create in all exercises, naming
conventions are extremely important to writing clear, maintainable application programs.

Template for a C++ program:

```
// programname.cpp
// author
// date

#include <iostream>
      ** other include statements may be required **
using namespace std;
      ** structs **
      ** function prototypes **
      ** constants **
      ** global variables **
int main()
{
      ** program statements go here **
      return 0;
}  // end of main function
```

You can use this template to begin many of your coding projects. A consistent look for all of your
programs shows good coding discipline. Using a proper structure, indenting, consistent use of
upper case and lower case can make your programming easier to debug for you and anyone who
needs to maintain your code at a later date.

Lesson 1.9 Summary

C++ is a widely used programming language which makes it an important language for a
programmer to master. The programmer should understand the steps to completing a C++
programming project as well as the way a C++ compiler goes about creating an executable file. A
good C++ program should be properly commented, spaced and indented mainly for ease of
maintenance. Good programming style usually indicates a well structured program.

End of Lesson Quiz

The plain text file that contains the C++ statements is called the _____ file.

The phase where the programmer breaks the problem down into logical steps is called the _____ phase.

You indent lines of code to increase _____.

CHAPTER 2
Problem Solving I

Objectives:

- Describe the tools available to plan a programming task.
- List the symbols used in flowcharting and their meaning.
- Explain how to use pseudocode to plan a programming task.
- Create an IPO chart to solve a programming problem.
- Define the steps in creating an IPO chart.

Lesson 2.1 Problem Solving

The ability to solve word problems is, perhaps, the most important tool in the programmers toolbox. Every program begins as a word problem. Someone expresses a problem either verbally or written, the programmer takes that information, analyzes it, develops the algorithm to solve the problem, and turns it into a working program or system of interrelated programs.

Often developing the algorithm is the hardest part of solving the problem. This is where the logic of programming becomes the "brick wall" in programming. Too often beginning programmers do not take the time to analyze the problem and try to develop a working algorithm "on the fly". This may work for the simple problems at the beginning but makes the more advanced problems more difficult.

This is why we devote some time at the beginning of this book to the mechanics of solving problems and using problem solving tools. Developing these skills at the beginning and following them throughout the course will make for a better learning experience.

Lesson 2.2 Tools

Now we need to examine some of the tools used to analyze word problems and produce the proper analysis of the programming problem to assist the programmer in producing accurate code. We will look at several of these tools: flowcharting; pseudocode; IPO Charts; and Documentation. While some of these have the same function, we will talk about each of them and as your expertise develops, you will learn which of these are best for you.

Lesson 2.3 Flowcharting

Once we have learned to break out a problem, it is often necessary to draw a picture of the process required to solve the problem. This picture is called a flowchart. It is a series of symbols connected by lines that depict the flow of the data to solve the problem. While there are quite a few different symbols that can be used, we will focus on a basic set of seven symbols that may be used to describe the flow of most programs.
- Terminal
- Process
- Decision
- Input/Output
- Page connector
- Off Page Connector
- Flow Line

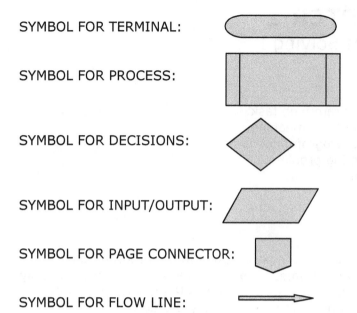

SYMBOL FOR TERMINAL:

SYMBOL FOR PROCESS:

SYMBOL FOR DECISIONS:

SYMBOL FOR INPUT/OUTPUT:

SYMBOL FOR PAGE CONNECTOR:

SYMBOL FOR FLOW LINE:

There are many more symbols but these are the important symbols for the purposes of this book.

SAMPLE FLOWCHART:

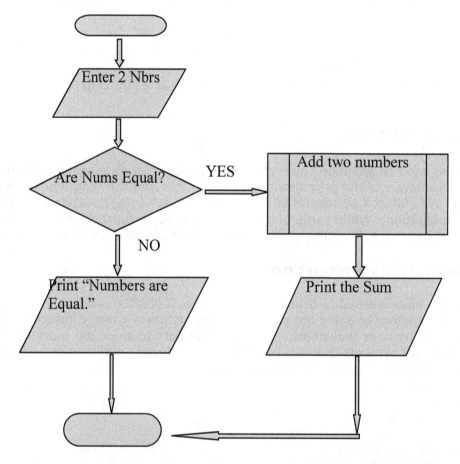

This flowchart represents a program that asks the user for two numbers. Then compares those numbers and if they are equal the program prints "Numbers are Equal". If the numbers are not equal, the program adds the two numbers and prints the sum.

For some programmers this type of visual representation is important to understand the flow of the code they will need to generate. It can be a time consuming process to develop a neat flowchart that is accurate. Often a flowchart is drawn in rough symbols on paper and then at the end, when all has been considered, drawn in a Word processor or with a flowcharting tool such as Microsoft's Visio or Dia (a free tool similar to Visio).

Lesson 2.4 Pseudocode

Pseudocode is another way to develop the logic of a program. It is merely writing down the steps to solve the problem in the correct and logical order. The process is similar to doing an outline before you write a report. It helps you organize your thoughts on writing the applications. There are no keywords or specific syntax for the pseudocode. Pseudocode for a problem requiring the solution to the simple interest algorithm, Interest = Principal Times Rate Times Term may be expressed in pseudocode as follows:

1. Ask the user for the principal amount.
2. Ask the user for the interest rate as a decimal.
3. Ask the user for the length of the loan in years.
4. Calculate the Interest by multiplying the principal times the rate and the result of that by the term of the loan.
5. Display the annual interest for the loan.

These simple sentences outline a step by step process for solving the algorithm.

Lesson 2.5 IPO Charts

Creating an IPO chart to analyze your program can eliminate many problems when you are ready to code. IPO is an acronym for Input, Processing and Output. Each letter represents a column in this three column form. First column lists the variables for the Inputs, the second column shows any processing items (variables created within the code) as well as the pseudocode or flowchart used to solve the problem. The third column list the variables that are to be output. There is a template for an IPO chart in Appendix B.

When using the IPO chart, you must first analyze the word problem and find out what is the goal or the output or the answer to the problem. That is, What is the answer we are looking for? When you discover what that is, write the goal in the output (O) column.

Next we look at the word problem and decide what is the algorithm or the formula to arrive at the answer we are looking for. Perhaps it is given as part of the problem or we may have to do some research for an algorithm that will solve the problem.

Now that we know the algorithm, we need to examine the word problem for input items. Has sufficient data been given to us to solve the algorithm or the formula or the equation we found to solve the problem? We need to make a list of all the inputs required, note those values that have been supplied by the word problem and place them in the Input (I) column of the IPO chart.

Then, back to the Processing column. Now we need to write the pseudocode or flowchart the processes required to solve the problem. These must be presented in the proper and logical order. First we need to gather any information required from the user that was not supplied by the problem. Next we need to plug all of the inputs into the algorithm. Finally, we need to display the output. If we need to create variables to hold the results of interim calculations that have not been listed in either the input (I) column or the output (O) column, we place those at the top of the processing (P) column in an area labeled (PI) for Processing Items.

Example:
Let's examine the following word problem:

Write a program to calculate the cost of the interest on a home improvement loan where a one year loan is secured at the rate of 5.85%. Ask the user for the estimate of the cost of the improvement and calculate the interest based on the amount entered into the program by the user at run time. How much interest will be paid?

Step 1: We need to discover the goal or the output for this word problem. The last sentence is the key, "How much interest will be paid?". Interest is the number we have to come up with. So, we write "Interest" in the Output (O) column of the IPO Chart.

Step 2: Next we should decide on the formula for calculating the interest on a loan. A little research will provide us with the formula: Interest is equal to the Principal amount of the loan multiplied by the rate of interest multiplied by the term of the loan. The actual formula is: $I = P * R * T$.

Step 3: Back to the word problem and see if we are given information about the Principal, the Rate and the Term. In the Input (I) column we need to put: Principal = user will enter, Rate = .0585, and Term = 1.

Step 4: Now we go back to the Processing (P) column and do the pseudocode for solving the problem.

1. Get user input for the Principal amount, rate and term of the loan.
2. Plug the inputs into the algorithm $I = P * R * T$.
3. Display the output (interest) on the screen.

It is a good idea at this point to practice using the IPO chart. You should practice several word problems using the IPO chart. This will be helpful in analyzing word problems and turning them into C++ programs.

Lesson 2.6 IPO CHART

All C++ program exercises and examples require an IPO chart prepared before beginning the code phase.

The IPO chart for the problem is shown below. It is important to map out how to solve the problem before beginning to write the code. An anonymous programmer once wrote: *"Weeks of programming can save hours of planning"*. Without a proper plan for your code it will take you many times longer to prepare a program than if you first took the time to plan your process to solve the problem and then coded it.

IPO Chart for Interest Problem:

```
      I(Input)              P(Processing)                        O(Output)
----------------+-------------------------------------------+--------------------
   Principle     | 1. Get the user to input the principle amount of  | Interest
   Rate          |    the loan.                              |
   Term of Loan  | 2. Get the user to input the interest rate.  |
                 | 3. Get the user to input the term of the loan.  |
                 | 4. Calculate the interest using the algorithm  |
                 |       Interest = Principle * Rate * Term  |
                 | 5. Display the output on the screen.      |
```

Lesson 2.7 Documentation

In the world of programming the dreaded question is "Where's the documentation?". Every programming project in the real world should be accompanied by some human readable content to explain various aspects of the program. We create IPO charts which certainly are a part of documentation, we insert comments into our code, another form of documentation but, we also need to provide a written narrative of the flow and technical details of the program.

Various programming shops have different requirements for such written narratives, and most expect this prior to the acceptance of the final product. If you are working for a company that writes commercial software, you would be expected to provide a user manual to explain how to use the product, an administrators manual to explain how to install and maintain the program and possibly a developers manual to help the programming department understand how to write programs to interface with the product or to alter the product to fit company needs. Then there should be a document that describes the various algorithms found within the program to insure the user knows how certain results were obtained from the input data.

Some companies will insist on training manuals and training materials to assist in bringing their workers up to speed on the program. Developers may keep track of the weekly progress of the development and the problems encountered in the development cycle. Also, we will talk about a series of test data that will be used to validate the results of the program during testing.

The word documentation strikes fear in the heart of many programmers. Programmers feel they are employed to write code not to write stories about their code. Many resist writing the documentation required and even to the point where they would rather leave their job than write documentation. Larger software companies have special documentation specialists to write the necessary documentation, but often it is left to the person who wrote the code.

Lesson 2.8 Summary

Programs are written to solve problems. Taking a "word problem", developing an algorithm to solve the problem, writing the code and finally testing and debugging the code is the mission. Some of the tools used to develop the algorithm are: Flowcharts, Pseudocode, and IPO charts as well as combination of these tools. If done properly, the coding, testing and debugging of the program will be much quicker and the documentation of the final program will be easier and more accurate.

End of Lesson Quiz

Every program begins as a _____ _____.

_____ is drawing a picture of the process required to solve a problem.

_____ is the written steps to solve the problem in the correct and logical order.

IPO is an acronym for _____ _____ _____.

CHAPTER 3
Problem Solving II

Objectives:

- Define the output required in a word problem.
- List inputs required by a word program.
- Create an algorithm to solve the word problem.
- List the steps needed to program a solution to the problem.
- Explain the importance of using IPO charts.

Lesson 3.1 Word Problems

In algebra we learned about solving for unknown variables like:

$$X = Y + Z$$

In this equation we assign the sum of the value of Y added to the value of Z to the variable X. So, if Y has the value 3 and Z has the value 2, the value of X will be 5.

$$X = 3 + 2$$
$$X = 5$$

We can translate this into a C++ program as follows:

```
// Algebra.cpp
// This is a sample program
#include<iostream>      // Required to read/write
using namespace std;    // Always required
int main()              // Always required
     {                  // Open Bracket Always required

// Declare Variables
// A variable is an unknown value
// Unknown at the time of programming but
// may be assigned an initial value that may
// or may not be changed.

int Y = 3;  // A variable named Y
            // with a value of 3

int Z = 2;  // A variable named Z
            // with a value of 2

int X = 0;  // A variable named X
            // with a value of 0

// Calculation
// X is assigned the value of Y plus the value of Z

X = Y + Z:

// The variable X now contains the sum of Y plus Z (5)
// and can be displayed
cout << "The answer is: " << X << endl;

return 0;   // Always required
}  // Closing Bracket - End of Main Function - Always required
```

The section of the program under // Declare Variables has three entries. We declare the variable Y and give it a value of 3, a variable called Z and give it a value of 2 and a variable called X and give it a value of 0 because we do not know the result of the calculation yet.

A variable is a chunk of memory that is allocated by the program to store a value. The value may, or may not, be known at the time the program is written. The value stored in a variable may be changed in the course of the program execution. You give that chunk of memory a name so your program can reference the correct area of memory to get the correct value for its calculation.

The section of the program under // Calculation shows the calculation of adding the amount stored in Y to the amount stored in Z and putting the result in the variable X. The expression to the right of the equal sign (assignment operator) is evaluated left to right and when complete, the result is stored in the variable to the left of the equal sign (assignment operator).

Lesson 3.2 Real World Example

Now, let's put a real life situation to this equation.

John has 3 Apples, Mary has 2 Apples, if they give all their apples to Mom, how many Apples will Mom have?

From this problem we develop an equation:
Mom's Apples = John's Apples + Mary's Apples

Our IPO chart should look like this:

```
          I                         P                               O
-------------------+-------------------------------+----------------------
Johns Apples = 3   |                               |   Moms Apples
Marys Apples = 2   |   add Johns apples to         |
                   |       Marys apples giving     |
                   |         Moms apples           |
```

Or in our example program from above:</p>

```cpp
// Apples.cpp
// This is a sample program
#include<iostream>
using namespace std;
int main()
{
// Declare Variables

int JohnApples = 3;
int MaryApples = 2;
int MomApples = 0;

// Calculation

MomApples = JohnApples + MaryApples:
// The variable MomApples has now been
// assigned the value of JohnApples plus
// the value of MaryApples.
```

```
// Display the result (MomApples)
cout << "Mom has " << MomApples << " apples" << endl;
return 0;
} // End of Main Function
```

We use exactly the same program but give the variables more explicit names. The program simply takes the values stored in JohnApples and the value stored in MaryApples, adds the values together and puts the sum in the variable called MomApples.

At the end of this process the contents of the chunk of memory assigned to each variable will look like:

Chunk called JohnApples =	3
Chunk called MaryApples =	2
Chunk called MomApples =	5

Lesson 3.3 A Complex Problem

Now we are ready to tackle an even more complex problem.

You purchase a new text book for $79.95 and the sales tax is 5%. You pay for the book with a $100 bill. How much change will you receive from this transaction?

Again we must first develop the formula or algorithm for solving this problem. It will really consist of several steps of formulas with the answer from one providing the data for subsequent steps.

We need a little more work on our IPO chart here to produce a chart that accurately reflects what we need to accomplish.

First, What is the output? We need to solve for the change received from our transaction.

Second, What are the inputs given? The price of the textbook $79.95. The rate of the sales tax which is 5%. Lastly, we pay with a $100 bill.

Notice that before we can solve for the change received we must know (a) the amount of the sales tax and (b) the total amount of the sale including tax. The storage areas for SalesTax and TotalCost are neither input or output. They are listed under Processing (P) as Processing Items (PI).

Next, we must solve for how much sales tax will be charged. This calculation is:

SalesTax = $79.95 times .05 OR
*SalesTax = PriceOfBook * TaxRate*

Next we need to find the total cost of our purchase.
TotalCost = $79.95 plus SalesTax OR
TotalCost = PriceOfBook + SalesTax

Last we need to calculate the change due from our $100 bill.

ChangeDue = $100 - TotalCost   OR
*   ChangeDue = Payment - TotalCost*

Our IPO chart should look like this:

```
     I                   PI(processing items)            O
------------------+--------------------------------------+-------------
                  |  SalesTax                            |
                  |  TotalCost                           |
                  |--------------------------------------|
                  |                  P                   |
------------------+--------------------------------------+-------------
PriceOfBook = 79.95 |   SalesTax=PriceOfBook * TaxRate    | ChangeDue
Tax Rate = .05      |   TotalCost=PriceOfBook + SalesTax  |
Payment = 100.00    |   ChangeDue=Payment - TotalCost     |
```

Our program will need more variables and three different calculations as we see above. Note the change in the IPO Chart. In the middle column there is a section marked PI (Processing Items). Processing Items are variables that need to be set up for interim calculations. They are neither input or output items. They are needed for storing the interim results of calculations in the course of processing. Hence the name Processing Items. In our example above, there are two processing items: SalesTax and TotalCost. As you can see looking at the three calculations, SalesTax holds the amount of Sales tax calculated and TotalCost holds the cost of the book plus the sales tax. Since the output is only the change due, these values are not considered output but are necessary to store the results of these calculation so that the ChangeDue can be calculated.

```cpp
// Change.cpp
// This is a sample program
#include<iostream>
using namespace std;
int main()
{
// Declare Variables
// Variables known from data in the problem
double PriceOfBook = 79.95;
double TaxRate = .05;
double Payment = 100.00;

// Variables that will be calculated in the
// course of running the program.
double SalesTax = 0;
double TotalCost = 0;
double ChangeDue = 0;

// Calculations

// Sales Tax Calculation
SalesTax = PriceOfBook * TaxRate;

// Total Cost Calculation
TotalCost = PriceOfBook + SalesTax;

// Change Due Calculation
ChangeDue = Payment - TotalCost;

// Display the change due
```

```
        cout << "Change: " << ChangeDue << endl;
        return 0;
    } // End of Main Function
```

In the calculations section we can see how we must order the calculations properly so the result is correct. First, we must calculate the sales tax. Next we calculate the total cost by using the price of the book plus the value we calculated for sales tax in the previous step. Last, we calculate the change due by taking the amount of payment and subtracting the value calculated in the total cost step. If these are done in any other order the result will be incorrect.

At the end of this process the contents of the chunk of memory assigned to each variable will look like the table below:

Chunk called PriceOfBook =	79.95
Chunk called TaxRate =	0.05
Chunk called Payment =	100
Chunk called SalesTax =	4
Chunk called TotalCost =	83.95
Chunk called ChangeDue =	16.05

Now you should understand why your ability to solve word problems is critical to understanding how to develop a computer program. You need to be able to solve the problem once, manually before you can teach the computer to solve the problem by giving it the steps, by which, you solved the problem correctly. Yes, a program merely teaches or instructs the computer to do things in the order dictated by the programmer.

Another point often missed by beginning programmers is the remarkable similarity of these small programs. Programs require that the programmer present the computer with directions in very specific order and syntax. There must always be a line:

int main() {

This opens the programs main function. This is how the computer knows where the instructions begin. Processing of a C++ program always begins at the main function. There must also be two lines at the very end:

return 0;
} // End of Main Function

This is how the computer knows when it is finished processing the main function of the program.

Everything between the curly braces must also be in a logical order. For your simple, beginning programs we can work with a template that will most often work for many of the programs you will be writing in the beginning. Then, as you learn the rules you can start to develop your own "style" of programming. However, be advised that in many programming shops you will be required to adhere to standards and styles of that shop and you may not be able to be as creative in style as perhaps you would like.

In our samples above, we first declared all our variables. This is important to do before the calculations because it tells the computer what the names of the variables are before the computer needs to use them. We certainly want to name the memory areas and load them with data before we do any calculations.

The second step of our programs was to do the calculation or calculations required to solve the problem. So, our template for all the examples above were a simple, two step, template to declare variables and then do calculations.

Lastly, we need to display the results of our calculations.

Now you are ready to move on to more complex problems and examples. To convert these problems into code it is often necessary to diagram the logic necessary for the computer to solve the problem. There are many tools to accomplish this task but we have discussed three of these and learned to use them to organize our thoughts. The three we have illustrated in this chapter are: Flowcharting, Pseudocode and IPO charts. Practice using these tools and it will help to insure your success in the remainder of this course.

Lesson 3.4 Why IPO CHARTS

Before beginning to code a C++ program, it is advisable to require an IPO chart be prepared to facilitate the code phase.

Organizing your word problems into IPO charts may seem to be a complete waste of time but, they do serve a vital service to the programmer. This is your road map to creating an efficient, well written program. It is not evident in the simple problems we have looked at so far, but in the not too distant future, you will be writing more complex programs and user-defined functions. The lack of an IPO chart will make your programming and debugging of these programs far more difficult.

Lesson 3.5 Sample IPO Chart and Program

PROBLEM:
Tom wants to borrow $1,000 for one year to purchase a new laptop. His bank will give him the money at twelve percent interest for one year. Tom wants to know how much interest he will pay on this loan.

IPO CHART:

I	P	O
Principal = 1000		Interest
Rate = 12%	Interest = Principal	
Term = 1	times Rate times Term	
	Display Interest	

PROGRAM:

```cpp
// Interest.cpp
// This is a sample program
#include <iostream>
using namespace std;
int main()
{
// Declare Variables
// Variables known from data in the problem
double principle = 1000.00;
double rate = 0.12;
double term = 1.0;
double interest = 0.0

// Interest Calculation
interest = principle * rate * term;
```

```
// Display the result
cout << "Interest on loan: " << interest << endl;
return 0;
} // End of Main Function
```

Lesson 3.6 Summary

Turning a word problem int an algorithm to solve the problem is often one of the most difficult tasks. First, you need to read the problem carefully and decide what information you need and what information you should throw out. If you can't solve the problem on paper, how will you write the code to solve the problem? The more complex the problem, the more complex the analysis and planning. IPO charts seem to be one of the best tools for assisting beginning programmers in organizing their analysis of a word problem.

End of Lesson Quiz

A _____ is a chunk of memory allocated by the brogram to store a value.

The computer starts to execute at the _____ function.

The programmer's ability to solve _____ _____ is critical to understanding how to develop a computer program.

CHAPER 4
Problem Solving III

Objectives:

- Explain the importance of a set of test data.
- Create test data for a program.
- Use test data for testing and problem solving.

Lesson 4.1 Test Data

Preparing to test your program is often a task that is completely ignored. However, this may be one of the most important steps in software development. Using a set of test data to test your program not only makes sure your program does what it was intended to do but also provides a means of conducting future tests after modifications have been made that insure you don't fix one problem and create a new problem.

A well crafted set of test data will test all of the possible values and conditions that the program is likely to encounter in the user environment. The test data should not only be good data but also data that tests the error handling of the program. You can count on the user entering a value that is out of range or the wrong data type. It is important that your program handle these errors and does not "blow up" on the user. Minimally, test data should test boundaries, one over a boundary, one under a boundary, and illegal data on each field processed.

Test data also comes into play when you make modifications to an existing program. You should be able to use the same test data to validate the changes you made did not affect the existing functions of the program. When you find a problem with a program and fix the problem that test data should be added to your original test data. The test data then becomes a document that grows as your application program changes.

Lesson 4.2 Building the Test Data

First step is to create a chart to track each input, calculation and output.. A spreadsheet is a great tool for keeping track of your test data and can be used to validate your calculations. The alternative is a paper version and hand calculate all your outputs. It might look something like this:

Principal	Rate	Term	Interest	Tests

The above form shows inputs and outputs for the Interest calculation problem. The user is asked for the three inputs and the output is calculated. To complete this form, enter a variety of responses for the three inputs, consider ranges, and invalid data. Once you have taken care of the inputs, using the algorithm for the calculation that we developed in our IPO chart, calculate the Interest for each set of input data. Where there is invalid data note that fact in the Interest column.

Lesson 4.3 Case Study

We will now apply what we have learned about IPO charts and test data to an actual program. We need to go though each step carefully and in order to develop a good plan for writing and testing our code.

Payroll

We will create a basic payroll program that will ask the user for the employee number, hours worked (maximum 40, minimum 8), rate of pay (maximum 25.00 minimum 6.35) and number of dependents (maximum 7). It will calculate the gross pay and the federal tax for the employee and lastly calculate the net pay and display the following: Employee Number, Gross Pay, Federal Tax, and Net Pay. Gross Pay is hours worked multiplied by rate of pay. Federal tax is calculated by taking gross pay minus $8 for each dependent times 15%. Net Pay is Gross Pay minus Federal Tax.

Let's create our IPO chart from the Payroll problem description:

First we are told that we need to calculate the Gross Pay, Federal Tax, and Net Pay for the employee.

Second we are told to ask the user to enter employee number, hours worked, rate of pay and number of dependents.

We are given the calculation for Gross Pay (hours worked times rate of pay); Federal Tax (15% of Gross minus $8 times the number of dependents) and Net Pay (Gross Pay minus the Federal Tax).

Let's apply this information to an IPO chart:

```
          I                          PI                                   O
---------------------+--------------------------------------------------+-------------
                     |                                                  |
                     +----------------------------------------------+   |
                     |                     P                        |   |
---------------------+----------------------------------------------+---+-------------
employee number      |  Get Employee Number                             | Gross Pay
hours worked         |  Get hours worked                                | Federal Tax
rate of pay          |      maximum 40 hours, min 8 hours               | Net Pay
number of dependents |  Get rate of pay                                 |
                     |      maximum 25.00 minimum 6.35                  |
                     |  Get number of dependents                        |
                     |      maximum 7 dependents                        |
                     |  Calculate Gross Pay                             |
                     |      hours worked times rate of pay              |
                     |  Calculate Federal Tax                           |
                     |      Gross Pay times .15 minus                   |
                     |         number of dependents times 1,000         |
                     |  Calculate Net Pay                               |
                     |      Gross Pay minus Federal Tax                 |
                     |  Display Results                                 |
```

Now we need to set up some test data. We should first create values for each input and then calculate each calculated value. When we run our program, we should get exactly the same results.

Inputs				Outputs			Tests
Emp. Nbr	Hrs. Wkd.	Rate of Pay	Dependents	Gross Pay	Federal Tax	Net Pay	
12345	40	10.75	2				Normal 40 hr pay
23456	40	9	0				Normal Pay No Dep
34567	40	10	8				Too many dependent
45678	40	30	3				Invalid Pay Rate
56789	45	10	0				Invalid Hours - Hi
98765	7	10	0				Invalid Hours - Lo
87654	40	25	7				All Max Values
76543	8	6.35	0				All Min. Values
65432	40	6	2				Invalid Pay Rate - Min

Test data should be prepared prior to starting the code phase. Preparing a table like we see above will help us understand the requirements of the programming phase. Thinking of all the possibilities is an exercise that may help clarify the code required to solve the problem.

Lesson 4.4 Maintenance

Once a program is in place, we must realize the world changes and requirements change. One of the companies that use our payroll system have a new requirement. We received the following request from their paymaster.

Payroll Change Request
Acme Corp. has decided to give all of our employees the opportunity to invest in a 401K program. We will allow them to put between 0% and 10% of their Gross Pay into a 401k program. We will deduct this amount pre-tax (before calculating the Federal Tax, this reduces the amount of federal tax paid by the employee). We also require the amount to be put in a 401K program be printed in the final report.

We need to go back and update our IPO chart appropriately to reflect the new changes. Yes, we should always keep our IPO chart as a form of documentation for our programs. Then we should look at our test data and add the appropriate columns and rows to reflect the new changes. Remember, these changes will affect our calculated fields so we will have to re-calculate each to insure proper test results. We will also have to add rows to reflect testing possible scenarios from adding this new requirement. I have shown the adjustments below.

Inputs					Outputs				Tests
Emp. Nbr	Hrs Wkd	Pay Rate	Dependents	401K	Gross Pay	401K Amt	Federal Tax	Net Pay	
12345	40	10.75	2	0.05					Normal 40 hr Pay
23456	40	9	0	0.05					Normal Pay No Dep.
34567	40	10	8	0.05					Too many dep.
45678	40	30	3	0.05					Invalid Pay Rate max.
56789	45	10	0	0.05					Invalid Hours Hi
98765	7	10	0	0.05					Invalid Hours Lo
87654	40	25	7	0.1					All max. values
76543	8	6.35	0	0					All min. values
65432	40	6	2	0.05					Invalid Pay Rate Low
99943	8	6.35	0	0					No 401K
99932	40	6	2	0.1					Max 401K
99921	40	6	2	0.12					Exceed Max 401K

Lesson 4.5 Importance of Test Data

All C++ program exercises and examples will require test data to be prepared before beginning the code phase.

The importance of test data is often overlooked. It helps us in a number of ways:
- To organize our thoughts on the program requirements.
- To think about input validation issues.
- To validate our algorithms by making the programmer hand calculate outputs.
- To insure changes do not adversely affect other calculations in the program.

So, it is important to take the time to learn how to generate test data. When you get a job in programming, it will more than likely require that you generate a complete suite of test data for your program projects and demonstrate that your code successfully solves all of the test data situations, both legal and illegal inputs.

Lesson 4.6 Summary

Too often a program is not completely tested before it is released to the users. Beginner programmers get into the habit that when it seems to run successfully, it is complete. Building a series of test data is necessary to test ALL of the possibilities before releasing to the users, they will find new problems. The test data will also be used to re-test the program when changes are made to the program to insure the change only affects the changed areas. When changes are made to solve the problem, new test data should be added to the series of test data.

End of Lesson Quiz

A well crafted set of _____ _____ will test all possible values and conditions the program is likely to encounter in the user environment.

Which is not an important issue for test data?
        Organize thoughts on program requirements.
        Demonstrate ability to use spreadsheets.
        Show validation issues.

Test data should be run on working programs when they are _____.

SECTION II - Basics

Lesson 5 - Data Types and Variables

Lesson 6 - Constants and Arithmetic Operators

Lesson 7 - Common Output

Lesson 8 – Common Input

Lesson 9 - Strings

Lesson 10 - File Input and Output

CHAPTER 5
Data Types and Variables

Objectives:
- Explain the concept of variables.
- List the rules for naming variables.
- Describe the uses of the various data types.
- Declare variables according to established rules.

Lesson 5.1 VARIABLES

Variables are names assigned to memory locations that may be changed while executing the program. The purpose of these memory locations is to hold data for the program to process. For example, if the operator enters the pay rate for an employee, the program needs a place to store this information for later processing. The programmer provides this space by "declaring" a variable (an area of memory) to store this data. When the programmer plans a program, he/she must also plan how many variables will be required by the program to do its work.

Variable names must be a combination of letters and numbers. A variable name must begin with a letter, contain NO SPACES or other special characters other than the underline character (_) and no C++ keywords may be used. It is also important to remember C++ variable names are case sensitive so MYPAY, mypay, myPay and MyPay are all different variable names.

RULES FOR NAMING VARIABLES

- Variable names must begin with a letter
- Variable names can contain letters, numbers and the underscore
- Variable names CANNOT CONTAIN SPACES
- Variable names must be less than 255 characters
- Variable name cannot be a reserved word
- Variable names CANNOT CONTAIN SPACES

Note the rule "Variable names CANNOT CONTAIN SPACES" is repeated twice. This is no mistake. This is one of the most common violations of the rules. If you need to include spaces in your variable names you can use the underscore character or use a method called "camelCase". The term camelCase is where you capitalize the first letter of the second word in a variable name. Example: Pay_Rate could be written in camelCase as payRate. Note the 'R' is capitalized in the second word.

Another subtle problem with variable names is that a variable name cannot be the same as a "reserved" word. Reserved words are words that are part of the C++ syntax. Some examples of reserved words are:
- cout
- cin
- include
- double
- float
- string
- if
- else
- while
- for
- loop

These are just some examples. For more complete information (See Appendix C).

These are also referred to as keywords. Generally these are all the words that make up the syntax of C++.

Long variable names lead to mistakes in spelling the variable names consistently and correctly. Keep your variable names short but descriptive. Remember, someone else may have to maintain your program so good naming conventions and good comments help to make your program easy to understand by other programmers.

Good Variable Names	Bad Variable Names
payRate	Pay Rate
two5	2five
raisePercent	Raise%
employeeNumber	Employee#
varFloat	float

Lesson 5.2 DATA TYPES

Each piece of data used by a C++ program must have a data type. When we reserve a piece of memory to store a value, we must also tell it what type of data we want to store there. Then when data is put into the storage location, it has the room to store the data and can reject the data if it is not of the correct type. The C++ language has some built in data types and also allows the programmer to create new data types as needed. For now, we will only work with the simple data types built into the system. The data types we will be working with are:

Data Type	Contents	Sample Value
int	An integer, a whole number	12
double	A floating point number, correct up to 10 decimal places	0.01
float	A floating point number, correct up to 6 decimal places	0.12
char	A single byte, capable of holding 1 character of data	'Z'
bool	Boolean value (True or False)	0 = True 1 = False

When do you use which data type?

Use the integer data type when dealing with whole numbers(numbers without a fractional or decimal part) 36 is a whole number. The internal rules of C++ will not allow you to enter any number with a decimal point. If you are entering a value that represents the number of students in your class, you would enter a whole number like 19. There are no fractional students, you can't have 18.5 students in a class. If you attempt to put 18.5 into an integer variable the 18 is stored and the .5 is truncated (NOTE: NOT rounded).

Use the double or float data type when dealing with numbers with a fractional or decimal part. Example: 3.14159 is a fractional number.

Use the char data type to store character data. This data type stores a number between -128 and +127. This range includes the ASCII values assigned to all the printable characters in the ASCII data set. Example: 'A' is a character with a ASCII value of 65, 'a' is a different character with a ASCII value of 97.

Use the data type of bool to hold a value for either TRUE or FALSE.

There are other data types but these data types are sufficient for our programs. Later in the course we will learn about some other data types.

Lesson 5.3 DECLARING VARIABLES

To declare a variable you must supply a valid variable name, a datatype and a semicolon. You may also assign a value at this time, this is called initialization.

Syntax for declaring a variable:

datatype variablename;

Selection of a data type for your variable is quite important. You must select data type based on the type of information you will keep in that variable and what operations you are going to use the variable for.
Example:
```
        int quantityOnHand;
        int numberUsed;
        double payRate;
        double bonusRate;
        bool decision;
        char response;
```

Note that I used "camelCase" in naming my variables to make short but meaningful names. Making your variables contents evident by selecting accurate names, helps in debugging and maintaining the program. Select your names carefully and it will pay dividends at debug and maintenance time.

It is important to note that C++ will automatically convert your data to the data type it needs to do certain arithmetic operations and this conversion may result in an inaccurate answer. This makes it necessary to look at your algorithms to insure you assign correct data types to each variable.

Lesson 5.4 INITIALIZING VARIABLES

When you declare a variable you reserve a space in memory to store some data. Sometimes we know there should be an initial value associated with that variable. So, when we declare the variable we assign that value to the variable. This replaces the unknown data in the memory with a known value. Any time you declare a variable it is a good idea to assign a value to that memory space, even if you just assign zero or a space.

The syntax for declaring a variable with an initial value is:
datatype variablename = value;

```
Examples:
        int quantityOnHand    = 0;        // variable initialized to 0
        int numberUsed        = 55;       // variable initialized to 55
        double payRate        = 10.55;    // variable initialized to 10.55
        double bonusRate      = 0.0;      // variable initialized to 0.0
        bool decision         = True;     // variable initialized to "True"
        char response         = 'Y';      // variable initialized to 'Y'
```

Lesson 5.5 CASTING (Type Conversion)

When we perform an arithmetic operation(next lesson) such as adding two numbers of different data types, for example, one of type integer and one of type double, the compiler decides on the data type of the output based on the datatype of the variable that will receive the value. This is called "implicit type conversion". The problem is that it may just drop the decimal part, without rounding or keep the decimal part, either of these may affect subsequent calculations and the validity of the answer.

To avoid this situation we use the cast operator to do type casting or type conversion so we can accurately predict the outcome of the operation. The syntax of the cast operator is as follows:

static_cast<dataTypeName>(expression)

EXAMPLE:(The result of this statement is answer will contain a decimal number)

```
double answer;
answer = static_cast<double>(10 * 3.14159);
```

The variable answer is created to hold a number with a fractional (decimal) part. The second instruction will multiply the integer 10 by the fractional number 3.14159. Since we are not sure of how the computer will store the answer we use the static_cast<double> to insure the result of the operation is a number that will include any decimal part. In this instance 31.4159 will be stored in the variable answer.

Lesson 5.6 SAMPLE PROGRAM

An example of a C++ program is shown below. The code shown declares five variables. It then adds the contents of two of the variables and stores the result in another variable. Then multiplies the contents of a type int variable by the a type double variable named PI, uses the cast operator to insure the result is a decimal number and stores the result in a variable.

```
// lesson5.cpp
// Date:
// Author:
#include <iostream>
using namespace std;
int main()
{
    // declare variables
    double PI = 3.14159;
    int firstnum = 5;
    int secondnum = 7;
    int answer1;
    double answer2;

    // processing statements
    answer1 = firstnum + secondnum;
    answer2 = static_cast<double>(secondnum * PI);
    // Display Results
    cout << "firstnum + secondnum = " << answer1 << endl;
    cout << "static_cast<double>(secondnum * PI = " << answer2 << endl;
    return 0;
}   // End of Main Function
```

The processing statements for this program consist of the following commands. First command adds the contents of the integer variable named firstnum (with a value of 5) to the contents of a second integer variable named secondnum (with a value of 7) and stores the result (12) in a integer variable named answer1.   The second command multiplies the contents of an integer variable named secondnum (with a value of 7) by the contents of a type double variable named PI (with a value of 3.14159). There are two possible outcomes for this multiplication. First it could be 31.4159, keeping with the rules of type double. Second, it could be 31, keeping with the rules of type int. To insure the program stores a type double answer in the type double variable named answer2, we need to do a static_cast<double> to force the answer to 31.4159.

Lesson 5.7 Summary

The concept of variables allow the programmer to name areas of memory to hold data for temporary storage or to use in calculations. It is important to understand the rules for naming these memory locations. Each programming language has its own set of rules.

C++ is a strongly typed programming language. This means that each memory location that is defined as a variable, can hold only the kind of data that was designated by the programmer. For Example, a variable declared to store data of type integer cannot hold numbers with decimals or character data.

It is not unusual to have mixed data types in a calculation. By this I mean, both integer data and floating point data may be part of an algorithm. To preserve the integrity of the solution it may be necessary to convert integer to decimal or vice versa. For this we use the static_cast.

Good C++ programming style dictates that variable names be in lower case or camelCase.

End of Lesson Quiz

Variable names must begin with a _____.

The term _____ _____ is where you create a variable name containing two or more words and capitalize the first letter of the second and any subsequent words.

Use type _____ or _____ when dealing with numbers with a fractional part.

Lesson 6
Constants and Arithmetic Operators

Objectives:
- Explain the construction and use of constants.
- Use comments in program code.
- List the arithmetic operators and describe their use.
- Use arithmetic operators in calculations.
- Use various assignment operators in calculations.
- Describe the precedence of operators.

Lesson 6.1 CONSTANTS

Constants are simply variables with values assigned that cannot be changed while the program is running. They follow the same naming rules as variables. Once a program starts to run, the value assigned to the constant cannot be changed. Constants are used for values to be used in programs that will never change. To change a constant, it must be changed in the source code and the program recompiled and linked. A good example is a program that uses the constant PI in its calculations. The value of PI is always 3.14159 (depending on how many decimal points required) and never changes.

The only difference between declaring a variable and declaring a constant is the use of the keyword "const" in the declaration.

Lesson 6.2 DECLARING CONSTANTS

To declare a constant you need only declare a variable, assign it a value (initialize it) and precede the whole statement with the keyword "const". When declaring a constant you must always initialize it to a value when declaring the constant.

```
Example:
        const double PI = 3.14159;
        const int MAX_PASSENGERS = 52;
        const char NEGATIVE_RESPONSE = 'N';
```

Note that I used "camelCase" in naming my variables but used all uppercase when naming my constants. This is a good way for you to look at your code and know if you are dealing with a variable or a constant when reading the code. Remember, a constant must always be initialized to a value.

Lesson 6.3 COMMENTS

Comments are statements written in your program that are not part of the program and are ignored by the compiler. They are used for putting documentation in your program. You use them to document what a particular statement does or how a group of statements are used. Comments always begin with two slashes (//) and everything after those slashes are considered to be comments all the way to the end of the line.

```
// Declare Constants (a comment line)
const double PI = 3.14159;    // This is a constant for PI
// Declare Variables (another comment)
```

Lesson 6.4 ARITHMETIC OPERATORS

A list of the most common arithmetic operators used in C++.

```
+       Addition
-       Subtraction
*       Multiplication
/       Division
%       Modulus
++      Increment
--      Decrement
```

Note that there is operator precedence in C++ and that in your formulas it is important to recognize that %, /, * are done before +, - and that arithmetic expressions are evaluated left to right.

Lesson 6.5 Calculations in C++

We use the arithmetic operators to perform math functions in the program code. Let's look at how we use each arithmetic operator.

In every instance, the arithmetic expression must either be stored in a variable, written to an output statement, or used as an argument for a function. Since we have not covered the last two yet, we will only be concerned with storing the result in a variable.

ADDITION (+):
This operator is used to add two numeric constant values or the contents of two variables that contain numeric values.

```
SYNTAX:
            variable = value + value;
```

```
EXAMPLE:
            answer = 3 + 7;
```

At the end of this operation the variable named answer should contain the value 10, which is the result of adding the numbers 7 and 3.

SUBTRACTION (-):
This operator is used to subtract a numeric constant values from another numeric constant value or the contents of two variables that contain numeric values.

```
SYNTAX:
            variable = value - value;
```

```
EXAMPLE:
            answer = 7 - 3;
```

At the end of this operation the variable named answer should contain the value 4, which is the result of subtracting the number 3 from 7.

MULTIPLICATION (*):

This operator is used to multiply a numeric constant values by another numeric constant value or the contents of two variables that contain numeric values.

SYNTAX:

    variable = value * value;

EXAMPLE:

    answer = 7 * 3;

At the end of this operation the variable named answer should contain the value 21, which is the result of multiplying the number 3 by 7.

DIVISION (/) (integer):
This operator is used to divide a numeric constant values by another numeric constant value or the contents of two variables that contain numeric values.

SYNTAX:

    variable = value / value;

EXAMPLE:

    answer = 7 / 3;

At the end of this operation the integer variable named answer should contain the value 2, which is the result of dividing the number 7 by 3. NOTE: there is no fraction or remainder as this is integer division and results in only the whole number which is reported with the remainder truncated. The answer in integer division is NOT a rounded number, the remainder is simply truncated.

MODULUS (%):
This operator is used to divide an integer numeric constant values by another integer numeric constant value or the contents of two integer variables that contain numeric values. The purpose of this command is to calculate the remainder (if any) from integer division.

SYNTAX:

    variable = value % value;

EXAMPLE:

    answer = 7 % 3;

At the end of this operation the variable named answer should contain the value 1, which is the result of dividing the number 7 by 3 which results in a remainder of 1. Modulus is commonly used to determine if a number is odd or even. An integer mod by 2 will return a 1 if odd a 0 if even.

DIVISION (/) (floating point):
This operator is used to divide a numeric constant values by another numeric constant value or the contents of two variables that contain numeric values.

SYNTAX:

    variable = value / value;

EXAMPLE:

    answer = 7.0 / 3.0;

At the end of this operation if answer is expecting a fraction (type double or type float) the variable named answer should contain the value 2.333, which is the result of dividing the number 7 by 3.

Now we can look at some code that uses variables in place of numeric constant values.

```
int num1 = 7;
int num2 = 3;
int answer;
double result;

// addition
answer = num1 + num2;   // answer will contain 10 after this operation

//subtraction
answer = num1 - num2;   // answer will contain 4 after this operation

//multiplication
answer = num1 * num2;   // answer will contain 21 after this operation

//integer division
answer = num1 / num2;   // answer will contain 2 after this operation (note no
fraction)

//floating point division
result = num1 / num2;   // answer will contain 2.333 after this operation

//modulus
answer = num1 % num2;   // answer will contain 1 after this operation
```

Lesson 6.6 ASSIGNMENT OPERATORS

Operators used to assign values to variables:

Operator	Example of Code	Result
=	num1 = num2	num1 receives the value of num2
+=	num1 += num2	num1 = num1 + num2
-=	num1 -= num2	num1 = num1 - num2
*=	num1 *= num2	num1 = num1 * num2
/=	num1 /= num2	num1 = num1 / num2
%=	num1 &= num2	num1 = num1 % num2

It is important to read the = operator as the assignment operator. The statement num1 = num2 is read num1 is assigned the value of num2.

```
int num1 = 0;
int num2 = 5;
num1 = num2;      // assigns vaulue of num2 (5) to num1   num1 now contains 5
num1 += num2;     // num1 now 10   (5 + 5)
num1 -= num2;     // num1 now 5    (10 - 5)
num1 *= num2;     // num1 now 25   (5 * 5)
num1 /= num2;     // num1 now 5    (25 / 5)
num1 %= num2;     // num1 now 0    (5 % 5)  5 divided by 5 results in
                  remainder 0
```

Numeric constants may be used in place of the variable on the right side of the expression.

```
num1 += 1;          // adds one (1) to the contents of the variable num1
num1 -= 1;          // subtracts one (1) from the contents of the variable num1
```

Lesson 6.7 OPERATOR PRECEDENCE

We generally perform arithmetic calculations from left to right just like we read a book. However, this is not always true in mathematics. All of our arithmetic operators have a sequence in which the should be performed. C++ uses this sequence to perform calculations. So, we must obey the laws of OPERATOR PRECEDENCE which states that certain arithmetic operations get performed before others.

Operator Precedence Chart:

OPERATOR	PRECEDENCE
!, +, - (unary operators)	first
*, /, %	second
+, -	third
<, <=, >, >=	fourth
==, !=	fifth
&&	sixth
||	seventh
assignment operator (=)	last

The equation 7 + 2 * 5 needs further qualification. If the equation is evaluated left to right and the addition is done first, the result would be 45. However C++ evaluates left to right but does any multiplication, division or modulus before addition and subtraction, so by those rules the answer is 17.

```
Example:

answer = 7  +  2  *  5
answer = 7  +  (2  *  5)       // How the computer calculates
answer = 7 + 10                // answer contains 17

answer = (7 + 2) * 5           // If you wanted the addition done first.
answer = 9 * 5                 // answer contains 45
```

There is precedence for all operators we have discussed. To do complex formulas or evaluations you must understand the complete concept of all operators in C++. See the Operator Precedence Chart for a complete picture of all operators and their order of precedence.

You may override the order of precedence by using parenthesis (). Examine the statements below to see how parenthesis can affect a calculations.

```
answer = 7 + 3 * 10            // answer is 210
answer = (7 + 3) * 10          // answer is 100
```

Two different answers for what appears to be the same data. The parenthesis make the difference. So, before you code your algorithm, understand how the order of precedence may affect the outcome.

Lesson 6.8 SAMPLE PROGRAM

An example of a C++ program is shown below. The code shown declares a constant and declares four variables. It then adds the contents of two of the variables and stores the result in another variable. Then multiplies the contents of a variable by the constant PI and stores the result in a variable.

```cpp
// programname.cpp
// author
// date
#include <iostream>
using namespace std;
int main()
{
    // declare a constant
    const double PI = 3.14159;

    // declare variables
    int firstnum = 5;
    int secondnum = 7;
    int answer1;
    double answer2;
    double answer3;

    // processing statements
    answer1 = firstnum + secondnum;
    answer2 = secondnum * PI;
    answer3 = answer1 / 2;

    // display results
    cout << "firstnum + secondnum = " << answer1 << endl;
    cout << "secondnum * PI = " << answer2 << endl;
    cout << "answer1 / 2 = " << answer3 << endl;
    return 0;
}    // End of Main Function
```

Lesson 6.9 Summary

Constants like variables are memory locations used to store data. However, constants may only be changed in the source code and cannot be changed at program run time. Constants should be named by the same rules as variables except that the name of the constant should be in uppercase to make it stand out in the code.

C++ like other programming languages are used to perform calculations. C++ supports all of the standard arithmetic operations.

Calculations in C++ are written on the right side of the assignment operator and the answer stored in the variable on the left side of the assignment operator. Standard operator precedence rules apply and may be overridden by the use of parenthesis.

End of Lesson Quiz

_____ are simply variables with values assigned that cannot be changed while the program is running.

_____ are statements written in your program that are not part of the program and are ignored by the compiler.

The Modulus operatore is the _____ sign.

The ____ is the assignment operator.

You may override the order of precedence by using _____.

Lesson 7
Common Output

Objectives:
- Use the cout statement in a program.
- Place decimal points in fractional output.
- Explain difference between fixed and scientific notation.
- Format numeric output.
- Describe good formatting practices.

Lesson 7.1 COMMON OUTPUT

To display output to the computer monitor you use the *cout* statement. The statement cout stands for **C**ommon **OUT**put. To use this statement you must use the include directive:

```
#include <iostream>
```

at the start of your program.

The cout statement sends information to the common output device which on the PC is the computer monitor. The syntax of the cout statement is:

```
cout << data to be output;
```

We use the keyword cout followed by the stream insertion character (<<), followed by the data to be displayed on the common output, terminated by a semicolon(;). We may use as many insertion characters, to separate parts of the output, as necessary to build our output string. The example below uses two insertion characters, the first to output the character string "Hello, World!" the second to output the manipulator *endl*. The endl manipulator causes the common output to direct the cursor to the first position of the next line. Some programers us the '\n' character to do the same thing.

```
cout << "Hello, World!" << endl;
```

This statement causes the phrase Hello, World! to be displayed on the computer monitor. The endl at the end causes the cursor to be moved to the beginning of the next line.

Consider the code below. It declares three variables and initializes two of the variables to 10 and 15 then, multiplies the two numbers and stores the answer in the variable named num3. It then continues on to display the answer and the contents of each of the variables.

```
int num1 = 10;
int num2 = 15;
int num 3 = 0;
num3 = num1 * num2;
cout << "Multiply num1 by num2 gives: " << num3 << endl;
cout << "or for the same result: " << num1 * num2 << endl;
cout << "num1 = " << num1 << endl;
cout << "num2 = " << num2 << endl;
cout << "num3 = " << num3 << endl;
cout << endl;
```

The output of this code segment would look like this:

```
Multiply num1 by num2 gives: 150
or for the same result: 150
num1 = 10
num2 = 15
num3 = 150
```

Lesson 7.2 FORMATTING

C++ provides the ability to place data formatting manipulators directly into the output stream. To use these manipulators you need to include the #include<iomanip> at the top of your source code. We will discuss several of these manipulators: setw(), setprecision(), fixed, showpoint. The fixed and showpoint do not require the iomanip directive, they are included in the iostream directive.

fixed - used to make sure the number is not displayed in scientific notation (example 1.034292e+004 would be displayed as 10342.92). Scientific notation is the computer's way of storing numbers that allows the storage of very large numbers or very small decimals. The number 1.034292e+004 translated means that when using the number move the decimal place 4 positions (e+004) to the right, resulting in 10342.92. If the number was 1034292e-004, this would mean that the decimal point should be moved 4 positions (e-004) to the left, resulting in 0.000134292 which is a small fractional number. Generally, this is not how we like to view our numbers in output so using the fixed manipulator corrects this problem for our printed output. So, in the future, if your output shows a number in scientific format, you now know how to fix that problem.

```
double sales = 13579.77;
cout << fixed;
cout << sales << endl;          //displays 13579.770000;
```

Where did the extra zeros come from? Fixed always displays a type double with 6 digits to the right of the decimal. We will learn to fix this later.

```
double num1 = 3.12345678;
cout << fixed;
cout << num1 << endl;           //displays 3.123457;
```

Note the decimal part was rounded up so that there are 6 digits to the right of the decimal.

showpoint - used to insure a decimal point is displayed with the decimal positions specified shown and padded out with zeros if needed.

setprecision() - this function requires:

```
#include <iomanip>
```

and will be used to determine the number of decimal positions shown. Include the number of decimal positions to be shown within the parenthesis. To have a number display with two digits to the right of the decimal point you would use: setprecision(2). Six digits to the right of the decimal point would be: setprecision(6).

```
double num1 = 3.12345678;
cout << fixed << showpoint;
cout << setprecision(2);
cout << num1 << endl;           //displays 3.12;
```

NOTE: The number displayed shows two positions to the right of the decimal.

```
double netPay = 987.6;
cout << fixed << showpoint;
cout << setprecision(2);
cout << netPay << endl;         //displays 987.60;
```

The setprecision function pads out the number to fill two decimal places.

```
double num1 = 3.12888;
cout << fixed << showpoint;
cout << setprecision(3);
cout << num1 << endl;        //displays 3.129;
```

This shows that the number to the right of the decimal is rounded properly to reflect a more accurate number.

setw() - allows us to specify how many columns our output will be allowed to occupy. Using setw() in your program requires that you include<iomanip> at the beginning of your program. If we have a number that must fit in 10 columns we would specify setw(10).

```
double num1 = 123.45
cout << fixed << showpoint;
cout << setprecision(2);
cout << "[" << setw(6) << num1 << "]" << endl; // displays [123.45]
cout << "[" << setw(8) << num1 << "]" << endl; // displays [  123.45]
```

All of your output should be formatted properly to make it readable. Nice, well organized output is always accepted as the creation of someone who knows what they are doing. Users always feel that someone who has paid attention to delivering a well formatted output, has also paid that type of detailed attention to the other internals of the program. They can read the output easily and don't look for problems that they would look for in a program where the output was "sloppy".

```
POOR EXAMPLE OF OUTPUT;

     gross pay:1234.56
           hoursworked:   40.0
        Rate of Pay10.00


WELL DESIGNED OUTPUT

        Gross Pay:      1234.56
        Hours Worked:     40.00
        Rate of Pay:      10.00
```

While both give the correct answer, the first example is hard to read, indicates someone who hurried through the project and reflects poorly on the designer. However, the second example demonstrates the work of someone who has pride in their work, has taken the time to design the output and the whole program will be viewed positively.

Now an example of using the setw() function in a program.

```
// setw.cpp
// Author:
// Date:
// Example Using setw() formatting

#include<iomanip>
#include<iostream>
#include<cmath>
using namespace std;
int main(){
        int x = 50;   //set the number you want to mark as end.
        int w = 12;   //set the width
        double sq;
```

```
        double cu;
    //set the column headings
    //use setw() with the contents of variable w for the width
            cout<<setw(w)<<"Number"<<setw(w)<<"Square"<<setw(w)<<"Cube"<<endl;
            cout<<"===================================="<<endl;
    //loop through
            for(int i = 5; i<=x; i+=7)
            {
                    sq = pow(static_cast<double>(i), 2.0);
                    cu = pow(static_cast<double>(i), 3.0);
                    //output the number, square and cube
                    cout<<setw(w)<<i<<setw(w)<<sq<<setw(w)<<cu<<endl;
            }
    system("PAUSE");
    return 0;
    }        // end of main function
```

Note how our example formats the output into columns of12 characters for both the headings and the results of the calculations.

Lesson 7.3 Debug Your Program

As you have probably already experienced, source code will not always compile. A missed semi-colon (;) or curly brace ({}) often cause errors. Variable names that are not legal variable names (example the name contains a space- Pay Rate instead of payRate) or you declared it spelled one way and misspelled it in the code. All of these and many others will prevent the compiler from compiling and running your program.

These errors are called syntax errors. These are the easy ones to fix. Most IDEs like Visual Studio and DevC++ have a debugger. This will point out the general area of the syntax error at compile time. Chances are it may even tell you exactly what is wrong with the code. However, sometimes the message is misleading. The syntax error may be interpreted as a different error or on a different line than what actually caused the problem. These error messages are often misleading. But, for the number of errors solved, the process is a big help in fixing syntax errors.

Once your program compiles and executes there is the potential of logic errors. These are more subtle and harder to find than syntax errors. A good example is where your program executes but does not calculate the output properly. This is where your test data comes into play. Sometimes you have to take the first test data line that does not compute properly and using this data play processor and go through your code step by step. Some IDEs have the capability of setting breakpoints during execution. This process allows you to tell the program to stop at various points in processing and display the contents of variables. Not all IDEs include this feature, so sometimes you have to do it the "old fashioned way".

A good file of test data is key in working the logic errors out of your program. The more conditions you anticipate and solve in your testing, the better your application will operate under production conditions. Once the user gets their hands on your program, they expect it to work without any problems. Nothing is worse for a programmer than to get back his program because it does not do something properly. Once the user finds an error the whole program is suspect and then everything will be questioned and the whole department may loose credibility.

Lesson 7.4 SAMPLE CODE

An example of a C++ program is shown below. This is a very simple payroll application program. It takes the hours worked, multiplies by rate of pay and outputs the gross pay to the common output device.

```cpp
// pay1.cpp
// Date:
// Author:
#include <iostream>
#include <iomanip>
using namespace std;
int main()
{
    // declare variables
    double hoursWorked = 40.0;
    double rateOfPay = 10.00;
    double grossPay = 0.0;

    // set format manipulators
    cout << fixed << showpoint;
    cout << setprecision(2);

    // processing statements
    grossPay = hoursWorked * rateOfPay;

    // display the results
    cout << "Gross Pay:    " << setw(6) << grossPay << endl;
    cout << "Hours Worked: " << setw(6) << hoursWorked << endl;
    cout << "Rate of Pay:  " << setw(6) << rateOfPay << endl;
    return 0;
}   // End of Main Function
```

The output of this program will look like this:

```
Gross Pay:    400.00
Hours Worked:  40.00
Rate of Pay:   10.00
```

Lesson 7.5 Summary

Once we have learned to calculate the answer to a problem, we need to display it for the user. C++ accepts data and displays data in streams of characters. To place a stream of characters on the default output device, we use the "cout" statement. We can use the cout statement to show the contents of a variable, a string literal, a numeric literal, the result of a calculation or some combination of these.

Formatting the output is accomplished by a series of data formatting manipulators. Fixed, showpoint, setprecision() and setw() are the most often used manipulators. Don't forget that several of these require that you include the <iomanip> directive.

Finding and fixing errors in code may be one of the most tedious tasks in programming. Usually the compiler finds the syntax errors and though the error messages may seem cryptic and misleading, they usually point the programmer to the proper area of the error. Logic errors are the more difficult to find and fix and often depend on having good test data to help manually step through the code to find the error.

End of Lesson Quiz

The statement cout stands for _____ _____.

The insertion operator is _____.

The _____ formatting manipulator makes sure the number is not displayed in scientific notation.

_____ allows us to specify how many columns our output will be allowed to occupy.

Lesson 8
Common Input

Objectives:
- Use the cin statement to accept data from the keyboard.
- Explain how to read a single character.
- Clear the input buffer with cin.ignore.

Lesson 8.1 COMMON INPUT

The cin statement (**C**ommon **IN**put) allows the user to enter streams of data on the common input device which is usually the computer keyboard. The cin statement allows the user to enter a number or a single character. The cin statement stops returning information when it encounters a end-of-line (return or enter key) or another "white space" character in the stream. The cin statement consists of the keyword cin followed by the stream extraction operator (>>) followed by a variableName where the input is to be stored (of the correct data type to hold the data entered) then ended by a semicolon(;).

```
cin >> variableName;
```

In the case where you have declared a variable of type integer and the operator enters a number, the data type integer will not accept anything other than 0 to 9, plus sign or minus sign and stops accepting data when any other character is typed.

If you enter 123,456.78 the cin statement returns 123 to the program because the comma is not an acceptable character. If you enter 123 A the cin statement returns 123 because it is stopped by the blank (a "white space character") between the 3 and the A. However if you enter 123.98 the computer will not recognize the decimal portion (.98) of the number and return 123 because integers cannot have fractional parts. Note that it truncates, it does not round.

In the case where you have declared a variable of type double and the operator enters a number with a decimal portion, it will accept the digits to the right of the decimal point because variables of type double are allowed to accept the digits 0 to 9, the decimal point, and the plus and minus signs. However if you enter the number 12,345.56, the variable can only accept 12 and stops at the comma which is an illegal character for the data type double.

If you enter "Hello, World!" the cin statement will only return "Hello" as the space stops the reading. Later we will discuss how to read strings into a string variable.

```
int num1;
int num2;
cout << "Enter a Number 1: ";
cin >> num1;
cout << "Enter a Number 2: ";
cin >> num2;
cout << "The sum is: " << num1 + num2 << endl;
```

This sequence will prompt you to enter two numbers. The first and second cin statements accept numbers, and store the numbers in the assigned variable. The cin statement stops accepting data when it encounters something other that a digit 0 through 9, a decimal point, a plus sign or a minus sign. In this instance it is waiting for the operator to hit the enter key before proceeding to the next prompt for the second number and then accepting the input of that number.

A single cin could be used to accept both numbers. The cin statement accepts only the digits 0 through 9 and a decimal point, a plus sign(+) and a minus sign(-). Any other characters are considered white space and white space characters signify the end of the input. Let's look at the same program as above using a single cin statement to accept two numbers with the same cin statement.

```
char response;
int num1;
int num2;
cout << "Enter two numbers: ";
cin >> num1 >> num2;
cout << "The sum is: " << num1 + num2 << endl;
```

In this program the operator is prompted to enter two numbers. The numbers could be entered by entering the two numbers separated by a space, by a comma or by the enter key. The data to be entered by the operator are in bold, the <Enter Key> notation is the Enter or Return Key on the keyboard.

ENTER:
      Enter two Numbers: **12 24** <Enter Key>
OR ENTER:
      Enter two Numbers: **12,24** <Enter Key>
OR ENTER:
      Enter two Numbers:**12** <Enter Key>
      24 <Enter Key>

Let's look at some examples of entering data using the cin statement:
The variables we used in this table have been declared as follows:
```
int num1;
int num2;
double numx;
double numy;
```

CIN STATEMENT	OPERATOR ENTERS	RESULTS
cin >> num1;	123	The integer variable num1 is assigned the value 123
cin >> num1 >> num2;	123 456	The integer variable num1 is assigned the value 123, num2 the value 456
cin >> num1;	123.78	The integer variable num1 is assigned the value 123
cin >> numx;	123.45	The type double variable numx is assigned the value 123.45
cin >> numx;	123	The type double variable numx is assigned the value 123.0
cin >> numx;	1,234.56	The type double variable numx is assigned the value 1.0
cin >> numx >> numy;	1,234.56	The type doule variable numx is assigned the value 1.0, numy assigned 234.56
cin >> numx;	1234.56	The type double variable numx is assigned the value 1234.56
cin >> numx;	10.00%	The type double variable numx is assigned the value 10.0
cin >> numx;	$123.45	The type double variable numx remains unchanged.

Examine each line in the above table carefully. Many problems with programs result from improper use of cin statements and their receiving variable data types.

Lesson 8.2 Reading a Character

Reading a single character can be done by using cin with the >> operator. However this is limited. It requires that a character be entered and ignores any leading white space characters. Simply the program will not continue past the cin statement until some character other than the space bar, tab key or enter has been pressed. If the program requires the user press the enter key to continue the cin >> will not do the job.

The solution to this problem is to use the cin.get() to allow the user to respond to a paused program by just pressing the enter key. Consider the following code sample:

```
char response;
cout << "The program has paused, Press the Enter key to continue";
cin.get(response);
cout << "The program now continues." << endl;
```

However, if we mix the cin >> and the cin.get() in a program we may encounter a problem. We will discover the fix in the next section. Look at the following code sample:

```
char response;
int num1;
cout << "Enter a number";
cin >> num1;
cout << "The program is paused, Press Enter to continue.";
cin.get(response);
cout << "The program continues" << endl;
```

This program will always allow you to enter a number but may not respond to the Enter key to continue the program. You may experience the program ignoring your output after entering a string of characters or input from a data file that looks correct is not inputting data the way it should be entered, etc.. This is a common problem in C++ when you are entering both string data and numeric data repeatedly. Go on to the next section to discover the fix to this problem.

Lesson 8.3 Using cin.ignore

Entering both string data and numeric data repeatedly or mixing the cin and the cin.get() instructions in the same program may cause unexpected values to appear in variables. To solve this problem we need to issue the cin.ignore() function. This function is used to clear out the input buffer to insure there is no residual characters from previous reads left in the buffer. The syntax for this statement is:

```
cin.ignore(n, c):
```

The 'n' is the number of characters to be cleared. Characters are cleared until the number of characters in the first parameter have been skipped or the 'c' character is encountered. Let's look at some sample code:

```
char response;
int num1;
cout << "Enter a number";
cin >> num1;
cin.ignore(100, '\n');  // clear 100 positions or up to the first '\n' character
cout << "The program is paused, Press Enter to continue.";
cin.get(response);
cout << "The program continues" << endl;
```

Any time you have a mix of numeric and character data coming into a program from the keyboard or from a file, you may need to use this function to periodically, clean up the buffer.

Lesson 8.4 Sample Program

A example C++ program is shown below. We have modified the code from the last lesson with the concepts we have learned in this lesson. The program declares the constant and variables but does not initialize any of the variables. The program then asks for two values performs the arithmetic functions and then displays the answer.

```cpp
// twonumbers.cpp
// author
// date
#include <iostream>
using namespace std;
int main()
{
    // declare a constant
    const double PI = 3.14159;

    // declare variables
    int firstnum;
    int secondnum;
    int answer1;
    double answer2;

    // get values from the user
    cout << "Enter an integer";
    cin >> firstnum;
    cout << "Enter an integer";
    cin >> secondnum;

    // processing statements
    answer1 = firstnum + secondnum;
    answer2 = secondnum * PI;

    // display the results
    cout << "firstnum + secondnum = " << answer1 << endl;
    cout << "secondnum * 3.14159 = " << answer2 << endl;
    return 0;
}    // End of Main Function
```

Lesson 8.5 Summary

To allow the user to communicate with the executing program the Common INput (cin) statement is used. The basic cin statement will accept a stream of data and store it in a variable. What is stored in that variable will be governed by the rules of that variables data type.

To store strings of data we need to use the cin.get(), this will allow the user to input strings of data that contain commas, spaces and other characters that may be rejected or it will also allow the programmer to just press the ENTER key without entering any data.

Using combinations of these input methods may result in data left in the buffer which may affect subsequent reads. To clear the buffer the programmer uses the cin.ignore() function.

End of Lesson Quiz

The statement cin stands for _____   _____.

The extraction operator is _____.

The solution to entering strings containing spaces from the common input is to use the _____ statement.

Use the _____ to clear the input buffer.

Lesson 9
Strings

Objectives:
- Explain the String data type.
- Use the getline() function to read string data.
- Copy data into a string using strcopy() function.

Lesson 9.1 Strings

The definition of a string is a group of zero or more characters. It is notable that characters are any of the ASCII (or Unicode) characters available for use by the computer. They include upper and lower case letters, digits and all special characters. Strings are a combination of these types of characters that can be read and stored by the string variable.

Note when we discussed data types there was no data type to handle a string of data like "John Dough". In our discussion of cin there is the fact that a space causes the input to stop. How then do we enter a string of data that includes spaces and other characters? Then, where do we store that input?

Let's start with the second question, how to store a string of data. This is accomplished with a new "Non-Standard" C++ data type called string. To use this data type you must include another header:

```
#include <string>
```

With this header you may now declare a variable of the data type string. The syntax of this variable declaration is:

```
string variableName [= optional value];
```

When we declare a string variable, we can declare it empty and available to store a string or we can give it an optional initial value. The last example below is showing a string named address2 that is initialized to a string of zero characters in length. This is known as a NULL string, Null meaning having no assigned value.

```
// declare variables
string studentName;          // declare a variable named studentName to hold string data
string custname = "John Doe";  // declare a variable named custname to hold string data and
                               initialize to "John Doe"
string address2 = "";        // declare a variable named address2 of 0 char in length, a NULL string
```

Now, the first question on how to enter data into this data type.

The first method is to simply assign data to the data type using the assignment operator. For example the instruction:

```
string customerName;
customerName = "John Dough";
```

This instruction assigns the value "John Dough" to the variable named customerName. Note when we enter a string literal in our program, we always enclose it in double quotes("). The compiler takes anything entered in double quotes and uses it as string data. However, the double quotes are not necessary when entering data through the keyboard.

We can also take the contents of one string variable and assign it to another string variable. For example the instruction:

```
string customerName = "John Dough";
string shippingName;
shippingName = customerName;
```

Assuming customerName holds the value "John Dough" at the end of this operation the variable named shippingName will also contain the string "John Dough".

There is another common input statement that comes with the string header included to process strings called the getline function:

```
getline(cin, stringvariable);
```

The getline function requires two arguments. The first argument is the source of the input which, in the above example, is the common input or cin. The second argument is the name of the string variable that will be used to accept the input.

```
EXAMPLE:
     #include <string>
     #include <iostream>
     using namespace std;
     int main()
     {
     string str1;
     string str2;
     cout << "Enter a complete sentence: ";
     getline(cin, str1);
     cout << str1 << endl;
     cout << "Enter a first name and a last name: ";
     getline(cin, str2);
     cout << str2 << endl;
     return 0;
     } end of main function
```

There are many other things we can do with strings that were not previously available in C++, like string comparisons. However, these are not part of this text.

Lesson 9.2 STRING CONCATENATION

At times we need to put combinations of strings and variable together on the same line. This putting one string or variable at the end of another string is known as concatenation. A few simple things to remember when composing your output line. First make sure you include a space between the end of the string and the start of the next component. Second, sometimes you need to start the next string after a variable with a space to insure the separation of the two components. See the examples below:

```
cout << "John " << "Dough" << endl;
cout << "John" << " " << "Dough" << endl;
cout << "John" << " Dough" << endl;
          DISPLAYS:   John Dough
```

```
netpay = 123.45;
cout << "Net Pay: $" << netPay << endl;
        DISPLAYS:    Net Pay: $123.45

firstName = "John";
lastName = "Dough";
cout << "Hello " << firstName << " " << lastName << " Welcome to C++ Class."
<< endl;
        DISPLAYS:    Hello John Dough Welcome to C++ Class.

Ticket - 12.99;
cout << "Ticket Price: " << ticket << endl;
        DISPLAYS:    Ticket Price: 12.99

num1 = 12;
num2 = 34;
num3 = 56;
cout << num1 << " " << num2 << " " << num3 << endl;
        DISPLAYS: 12 34 56

name = "Dough";
payRate = 10.00;
hrsWkd = 40.00;
netPay = 400.00;
outFile << name << ";" << payRate << ";" << hrsWkd << ";" << netPay << endl;
        DISPLAYS: Dough;10.00;40.00;400.00
```

Note the placement of spaces either in the string literals of as a separate character within the command structure. If you neglect to put in the spaces it may be hard to decipher the output.

Lesson 9.3 SAMPLE CODE

An example C++ program is shown below. We have modified the code from the last lesson with the concepts we have learned in this lesson. The program now asks for the employee name and stores it in a variable called "name". Then at the end it prints a message with the employee name embedded.

```cpp
// pay1.cpp
// Jim Kelley
// 6 November 2007
#include <iostream>
#include <iomanip>
#include <string>
using namespace std;
int main()
{
    // declare variables
    double hoursWorked = 0.0;
    double rateOfPay = 0.00;
    double grossPay = 0.0;
    string name;

    // set format manipulators
    cout << fixed << showpoint;
    cout << setprecision(2);

    // Enter employee first and last name
    cout << "Enter Employee Name: ";
```

```
        getline(cin, name);

        // Ask the user for the inputs
        cout << "Enter the hours worked ";
        cin >> hoursWorked;

        cout << "Enter the rate of pay ";
        cin >> rateOfPay;

        // processing statements
        grossPay = hoursWorked * rateOfPay;

        // display the result
        cout << "Weekly Pay for: " << setw(6) << name << endl;
        cout << "Gross Pay:      " << setw(6) << grossPay << endl;
        cout << "Hours Worked:   " << setw(6) << hoursWorked << endl;
        cout << "Rate of Pay:    " << setw(6) << rateOfPay << endl;
        return 0;
    }
```

The output of this program will look like this:

```
    Weekly pay for: John Doe
    Gross Pay:      400.00
    Hours Worked:    40.00
    Rate of Pay:     10.00
```

Lesson 9.4 Summary

Data comes into C++ as streams of characters. Simple data types like int, double, char, bool have simple rules for the limited number of characters they can accept. When it comes to strings, there are a large number of characters, spaces must be allowed and the length of the string is, in itself another variable. In C and older versions of C++ this was handled by an array of data type char. The 1998 ANSI/ISO changes allowed for a new "string" data type. To use this data type you will need to include the <string> directive in your program.

Since the cin stops filling the buffer when it sees a space, another means of input is needed. The best for inputting strings is the getline() function. This accepts string data from the common input or a file and places the string in the indicated variable.

Sometimes we need to put combinations of strings and variables next to each other on the same line. This is called "concatenation". This is usually accomplished with one of the output statements.

End of Lesson Quiz

The definition of a _____ is a group of zero or more characters.

The getline function requires _____ arguments.

Joining one string or variable at the end of another string or variable is known as _____.

Lesson 10
File Input and Output

Objectives:
- Read data into program from text files.
- Write output to a text file.
- Create text files for input with Notepad.
- Use Notepad to view files created by the program

Lesson 10.1 FILE INPUT / OUTPUT

Writing your data to files is an important part of processing data. C++ has several requirements to set up reading or writing files. C++ writes files in streams of data. So, like other operations we need to include the directives that handles streams of data. We need to include:

```
#include<fstream>
```

This must be placed with the other include directives at the top of the program.

Lesson 10.2 FILE INPUT

Next we need to tell the program the name of the file and if it is input or output. To declare and open an input file we need two steps. The first step is to assign a variable name to the input file. This name will be used each time the program needs to refer to this particular input file. In our examples we have used *inputFilename* as a name. This can be any name that helps to identify the particular data found in the file. Once again be as descriptive as possible.

The second step is to issue the open function to allow the program to find the input file and open it for use in the program.

For input we use the statements:

```
ifstream inputFilename;
inputFilename.open("C:\\file.ext");
```

To read data from an input file:
```
inputFilename >> field1;
```

When finished, remember to close the file as good practice:

```
inputFilename.close();
```

Sample Code:

```
EXAMPLE:
    #include <fstream>                  // required to read files
    #include <string>
    #include <iostream>
    using namespace std;
    int main()
    {
        double hours = 0.0;
```

```
        double rate = 0.0;

        ifstream myFile;              // declare an input file variable
        myFile.open("infile.txt");    // open a file
        myFile >> hours;                  // read in the first field
        myFile >> rate;                   // read in the second field
        myFile.close();                   // close the file
        cout << hours << endl;
        cout << rate << endl;
        return 0;
}    // End of Main Function
```

Lesson 10.3 FILE OUTPUT

To declare and open an output file we need two steps. The first step is to assign a variable name to the output file. This name will be used each time the program needs to refer to this particular output file. In our examples we have used *outputFilename* as a name. This can be any name that helps to identify the particular data to be placed in the file. Once again be as descriptive as possible.

The second step is to issue the open function to allow the program to find the output file and open it for use in the program.

For output we use the statements:

```
        ofstream outputFilename;
        outputFilename.Open("file.ext");
```

To write to an output file we may use a statement like this:

```
        outputFilename << field1 << field2 << '\n';
```

When finished, remember to close the file as good practice:

```
        outputFilename.close();
```

Here is how you use this code to generate an ouput file:

```
EXAMPLE:
    #include <fstream>
    #include <string>
    #include <iostream>
    using namespace std;
    int main()
    {
        ofstream myFile;
        myFile.open("outfile.dat");
        myFile << "The quick brown fox \n";
        myFile << "Jumped over the lazy brown dog \n";
        myFile.close();
        return 0;
}    // End of Main Function
```

There is also an optional mode argument that can be used after the data identifier called the mode. This allows the programmer to specify how to open a file. This is especially important for the output files. When you open an output file without the mode identifier you delete any existing contents of the output file. If you want to open an output file and add to the existing contents you will need to specify the mode as (ios::app). This will place the write point immediately after the last existing record in the file.

List of file modes used with files:

filename.Open("file.dat", mode);

MODE	OPERATION
ios::out	Open a file to write a record. If the file exists it overwrites existing data, if the file does not exist it creates a new file.
ios::in	Open a file to input records
ios::app	Open a file to add to existing records. If the file exists it adds the next record after the last record. If the file does not exist, it creates a new file.

Lesson 10.4 Using both input and output files in a program

Often it will be necessary to have both input and output files in a program. Sometimes you will have multiple input and multiple output files in a program. The next sample program will open two input files and two output files. One output file will create a new file each time, the other will append to existing records.

```
EXAMPLE:
        #include <fstream>
        #include <string>
        #include <iostream>
        using namespace std;
        int main()
        {
                // Declare Some Variables
                int field1, field2, field3, field4;

                // Declare and open the input and output files
                ifstream inFileOne;
                ifstream inFileTwo;
                ofstream outFileNew;
                ofstream outFileAppend;
                inFileOne.Open("fileone.txt", ios::in);
                inFileTwo.Open("filetwo.txt", ios::in);
                outFileNew.Open("outnew.dat", ios::out);
                outFileAppend.Open("outappend.dat", ios::app);

                // Read data from both input files
                inFileOne >> field1 >> field2;
                inFileTwo >> field3 >> field4;

                // Write data to both output files
                outFileNew << field1 << field2 << field3 << field4 << endl;
                outFileAppend << field1 << field2 << field3 << field4 << endl;

                // Close all files
                inFileOne.close();
                inFileTwo.close();
                outFileNew.close();
                outFileAppend.close();
```

```
            return 0;
    }      // End of Main Function
```

Using a text editor, create the following 4 files (See Lesson 10.5) to test the program: (file values are bold)

INPUT FILES:
```
        fileone.txt
```
12 24 36 48

```
        filetwo.txt
```
100 500 1000 1500

```
        outnew.dat
```
11 22 33 44

```
        outappend.dat
```
111 333 555 777

When the program finishes the two output files should contain the following data:

OUTPUT FILES:
```
        outnew.dat
        12  24  36  48

        outappend.dat
        111  333  555  777  100  500  1000  1500
```

Both output files (outnew.dat and outappend.dat) contain data. The outnew.dat file is opened as an output file (ios::out). Although it already contains data, the data is overridden. The outappend.dat file is opened as an append output file (ios::app). The new data is written to the file after the last existing record on the file.

Lesson 10.5 Creating Input Files with Notepad (or any other text editor)

To create input files for our programs you need a text editor. The Notepad program that comes with all versions of Windows is an excellent choice. We will use Notepad for creating input files for all examples in this course. Notepad puts an extension of .txt on all files that it creates.

To create a file, open notepad and enter the text and when you are done, select the destination for writing the file, name the file and click on the save button.

Lesson 10.6 Reading Output Files with Notepad (or any other text editor)

Reading text files is a little trickier. Sometimes text files do not have the standard extension .txt at the end. So, we must "Right Click" on the file and in the pop up menu, select "Open With" this produces a dialog box where one of the selections is Notepad. Select Notepad and click on OK and the file will open in notepad.

Lesson 10.7 SAMPLE PROGRAM

We continue improving our payroll program. This version will take the input from a plain text file and output the report to a plain text file. The calculation will remain the same but compare the input and output statements to the prior examples.

Using Notepad or other text editor, create a file named **payin.txt** that contains the following one line of information:

```
40.0 10.00 John Dough
```

```cpp
// pay1.cpp
// Date:
// Author:
#include <iostream>
#include <iomanip>
#include <string>
#include <fstream>

using namespace std;
int main()
{
        // declare variables
        double hoursWorked = 40.0;
        double rateOfPay = 10.00;
        double grossPay = 0.0;
        string name;

        // declare input and output file streams
        ifstream inFile;
        ofstream outFile;

        // open the files for input and output
        inFile.open("payin.txt");
        outFile.open("payroll.dat");

        // set format manipulators
        cout << fixed << showpoint;
        cout << setprecision(2);

        // Ask the user for the inputs

        inFile >> hoursWorked;

        inFile >> rateOfPay;

        getline(inFile, name);

        // processing statements
        grossPay = hoursWorked * rateOfPay;

        // display the result
        outFile << "Weekly Pay for: " << setw(6) << name << endl;
        outFile << "Gross Pay:      " << setw(6) << grossPay << endl;
        outFile << "Hours Worked:   " << setw(6) << hoursWorked << endl;
        outFile << "Rate of Pay:    " << setw(6) << rateOfPay << endl;

        inFile.close();
        outFile.close();

        return 0;
}       // End of Main Function
```

The output of this program will be in C:\payroll.dat and look like this:

```
Weekly pay for: John Dough
Gross Pay:      400.00
Hours Worked:    40.00
Rate of Pay:     10.00
```

Lesson 10.8 Summary

Programs designed to process large amounts of data usually get their input from files and output results to other files or add to the existing file. File processing requires that the <fstream> directive be included, A variable name for the stream (input or output) be declared, the file must be opened to read or write data and at the end, the file must be closed. The instructions to read and write data are similar to the cin and cout statements used for common input and output.

In this course we will only address text files as input and output. To generate an input file a text editor like notepad, notepad++ or any word processor that can output text files is needed. These programs can both create and read text input and output.

End of Lesson Quiz

The first step in opening an input file is to assign a _____ _____ to the input file.

If you want to open an output file and add to the existing contents, you need to specify the mode as _____.

Using the mode _____ will overwrite any data in an existing file of that name or create a new file if a file with the name specified does not exist.

SECTION III - Decisions

Lesson 11
Decisions - Simple If Statement

Objectives:
- Use a single sided IF statement in a program.
- Explain relational operators.
- List the relational operators.

Lesson 11.1 Decisions

Sometimes it is necessary for a program to evaluate an expression and based on the result, of an expression and if it evaluates to true, execute some alternate code. An example of such a decision is a program has accepted an input from the keyboard. The input requested was an integer greater than 0. A decision statement is written to test and determine if the data entered is not a valid integer. If this condition is true, the program will inform the user and terminate. If the condition evaluates as false (the date entered is valid) the program will continue.

The expression to be evaluated is written to compare two operands using a relational operator. The operands may be variables, constants, or literals.

EXAMPLE:

```
a = 5;
if (a == 5)
{
      true statements;
}
cout << a;
```

In the example, the variable is initialized to 5. The if statement evaluates the expression (a == 5). If the contents of a is equal to 5 the evaluation is true and the block of statements in the if statement will be executed and the program will continue with the statement after the closing bracket. If the contents of the variable a is not equal to 5 the program will continue with the statement after the closing bracket that outputs the content of the variable a to the common output.

Lesson 11.2 Relational Operators

There are six (6) Relational operators.

```
==          EQUAL
!=          NOT EQUAL
<           LESS THAN
>           GREATER THAN
<=          LESS THAN OR EQUAL TO
>=          GREATER THAN OR EQUAL TO
```

Relational operators are used to compare two operands and return a true or false answer. Constructing the expressions using relational operators are key in developing If statements.

There are several combinations of operands that may be compared:

- Compare two numeric literals. A typical comparison would look something like: (3 <= 7).
- Compare a numeric literal with the contents of a variable: (3 < students)
- Compare the contents of two variables: (students > minstudents)

- Compare a numeric literal with the results of an expression: (2 == 4/2)
- Compare the contents of a variable with an expression: (maxpay < hours * payrate)
- Compare the contents of a character variable with a character literal: (response == 'Y'

I'm sure there are other combinations but this should give you some idea of the comparisons you can make. Note we did not do any string comparisons, that is another topic covered in another lesson. For now, we will not do that type of comparison.

```
8 == 8        Evaluates to True      8 == 7      Evaluates to False
8 != 8        Evaluates to False     8 != 7      Evaluates to True
8  < 8        Evaluates to False     8  < 9      Evaluates to True
8  > 8        Evaluates to False     9  > 8      Evaluates to True
8 <= 8        Evaluates to True      8 <= 9      Evaluates to True
8 >= 8        Evaluates to False     9 >= 8      Evaluates to True
'A' == 'a'    Evaluates to False    'b' > 'a'    Evaluates to True
```

The simple If statement evaluates an expression and executes certain statements if the expression evaluates to true. For example, the expression may be the comparison of two constants like (3 > 1). Since three is greater than one this expression evaluates to true. The true statements are executed and then the program continues. If the expression evaluates to false those true statements are skipped and the program continues.

An expression may also evaluate the contents of two variables. In the example where we have an integer variable named varone that contains the number 5 and a second integer variable named vartwo that contains the number 5 and we compare these two variables (**varone == vartwo**), the result is true since 5 is equal to 5.

Lesson 11.3 SIMPLE IF STATEMENT

This statement is used to make simple decisions based on evaluating an expression that evaluates to either true or false. The simple IF statement evaluates a Boolean expression, performs one or more statements, if the evaluation is true or continues with the next statement if false.

```
if (evaluation expression) {code to be executed if true;}
```

Now let us look at using this code to make a decision and if the decision is true it will execute the following statement. If the decision is false it will execute the following instruction.

```
EXAMPLE:
    if (3 > 15)
          cout << "The expression evaluated true" << endl;
          cout << "This is the instruction after the simple if statement." << endl;
          return 0;
```

The if statement tests FALSE (3 is not greater than 15). The next statement is the single true statement for the if statement so it is skipped and the following instruction places the string "This is the instruction after the simple if statement." is placed on the common output. Lastly, the return statement is executed.

In the instance where the decision is true and several statements need to be executed, the statements must be enclosed in a set of curly braces.

```
EXAMPLE:
if (3 > 15)
   {
```

```
        cout << "The expression evaluated true" << endl;
        cout << "The second line of the true decision" << endl;
    }
        cout << "This is the instruction after the simple if statement." << endl;
return 0;
```

The if statement tests FALSE (3 is not greater than 15). The curly bracket indicates there is a statement block, a group of statements to be executed only if the expression is true. All statements within the set of curly braces are skipped since the evaluation was false. Finally, the instruction after the closing curly brace is executed and places the string "This is the instruction after the simple if statement." on the common output. Lastly, the return statement is executed.

Lets look at some code to illustrate using relational operators and variables.

```
int num1 = 6;
int num2 = 15;

if (num1 < num2)
    cout << num1 << " is less than " << num2 << endl;
```

The variable num1 is initialized to 6 and num2 is initialized to 15. Then in the if statement the contents of num1 and num2 are compared. If the contents of num1 is less than the contents of num2 the expression is true and the true statement will be executed. Since there is only one statement to be executed if the condition is true, there is no need for enclosing it in brackets.

Lesson 11.4 Sample Code

A sample C++ program is shown below. We have modified the code from the last lesson with the concepts we have learned in this lesson. We need to calculate the federal tax based on 12% for those who earn 400.00 per week or less and 18% on those who earn more than 400.00 per week. To accomplish this we need to add a decision. We will examine the contents of the variable "grosspay" and if it is less than or equal to 400.00 we do the calculation of assigning the result of multiplying grossPay by 12% to the variable fedTax. The next decision is to examine the contents of the variable "grosspay" and if it is greater than 400.00 we do the calculation of assigning the result of multiplying grossPay by 18% to the variable fedTax. Then we can calculate the netPay by subtracting fedTax from grossPay

In the pay1 exercise you are to create an input file from which the program will get its input. Create this file using notepad and name it: payin.txt (the name must be exactly like this) Put the file in your pay1/pay1 project folder. With the pay1.cpp file.

Input File for Sample: 40.0 10.00 John Dough

```
// pay1.cpp
// Date:
// Author:
#include <iostream>
#include <iomanip>
#include <string>
#include <fstream>

using namespace std;
int main()
{
    // declare variables
    double hoursWorked = 0.0;
    double rateOfPay = 0.00;
```

```cpp
        double grossPay = 0.0;
        string name;
        double fedTax = 0.0;
        double netPay = 0.0;

        // declare input and output file streams
        ifstream inFile;
        ofstream outFile;

        // open the files for input and output
        inFile.open("payin.txt");
        outFile.open("payroll.dat");

        // set format manipulators
        cout << fixed << showpoint;
        cout << setprecision(2);

        // Get inputs from payin.txt
        inFile >> hoursWorked;
        inFile >> rateOfPay;

        getline(inFile, name);

        // processing statements
        grossPay = hoursWorked * rateOfPay;

        // decide how much federal tax the employee should pay
        // next 4 lines: demonstrate the single sided if statement
        if (grossPay <= 400.00)
            fedTax = grossPay * .12;
        if (grossPay > 400.00)
            fedTax = grossPay * .18;

        // calculate the net pay
        netPay = grossPay - fedTax;

        // display the result
        outFile << "Weekly Pay for: " << setw(6) << name << endl;
        outFile << "Gross Pay:      " << setw(6) << grossPay << endl;
        outFile << "Hours Worked:   " << setw(6) << hoursWorked << endl;
        outFile << "Rate of Pay:    " << setw(6) << rateOfPay << endl;
        outFile << "Federal Tax:    " << setw(6) << fedTax << endl;
        outFile << "Net Pay:        " << setw(6) << netPay << endl;
        inFile.close();
        outFile.close();
        return 0;
}       // End of Main Function
```

If your program is successful, the output file will be found in the same folder and can be read with notepad, just like any other text file.

The output of this program will be named payroll.dat and look like this:

```
    Weekly pay for: John Dough
    Gross Pay:      400.00
    Hours Worked:    40.00
    Rate of Pay:     10.00
    Federal Tax:     48.00
    Net Pay:        352.00
```

Lesson 11.5 Summary

The simple if statement or decision statement, allows for the evaluation of an expression or set of expressions and on evaluation to true, do a statement or block of statements. If the expression evaluates to false skips that instruction or block of instructions and continues executing the program.

The C++ programmer should be familiar with the six basic relational operators and understand how they are evaluated and written in code.

End of Lesson Quiz

There are _____ relational operators.

The _____ statement is used to make simple decisions based on evaluating an expression that evaluates to True or False.

The relational operator for equality is _____

Lesson 12
Decisions - If...Else Statement

Objectives:
- Write code for If...Else statements.
- Explain logical operators.
- Use Nested If...Else Statements.
- Describe uses of If...Else statements.

Lesson 12.1 IF....ELSE STATEMENT

In instances where it is necessary to do different statement blocks based on an expression evaluating true or false you will need to use the if..else statement.   If the expression evaluates to true, the first block of statements are executed. If the expression evaluates to false the block of statements after the else statement are executed. The syntax of the if...else statement is shown below:

```
if (evaluation expression)
    {
        True statement block
    code to be executed if true;
    }
else
    {
        False statement block
    code to be executed if false;
    }
```

In the following example we will compare the contents of the variables named num1 and num2. If the contents of num1 is greater than the contents of num2 we will subtract num2 from num1. If they are equal or num1 is less than num2, num1 is subtracted from num2. The results are assigned to a variable named num3 and finally printed to the screen. Since we are using subtraction we want to subtract the smaller number from the larger number so we do not result in negative numbers.

EXAMPLE:

```
int num1;
int num2;
int num3;
cout << "Enter First Number: ";
cin >> num1;
cout << "Enter Second Number: ";
cin >> num2;
if (num1 > num2)
{
      num3 = num1 - num2
}
else
{
      num3 = num2 - num1
}
cout << "The result is: " << num3 << endl;
```

If the user entered a 5 for the first number and a 3 for the second number the evaluation of the contents of num1, a 5 is greater than the contents of num2 a 3, this evaluates to true. So, the contents num2 is subtracted from the contents of num1 (5 – 3) and a 2 is stored in the variable named num3.

If the user entered a 3 for the first number and a 5 for the second number, the evaluation of the contents of num1, which is a 3 is greater than the contents of num2 a 5, this evaluates to false. So, the contents of num1 is subtracted from the contents of num2 (5 – 3) and a 2 is stored in the variable named num3.

Lesson 12.2 NESTED IF....ELSE STATEMENT

An if statement block may contain other if statements. These are called nested if statements.

Nesting If...Else statements means that you put another If...Else statement within the true side or the false side of another If...Else statement.

EXAMPLE OF NESTED IF STATEMENTS

```
int age = 0;
char registered = 'Y';
cout << "Enter your age:   ";
cin >> age;
cout << "Are you registered to vote Y or N:   ";
cin >> registered;
If (age >= 18)
    {
    If (registered == 'Y')              // The Nested If...Else statement
        {
        cout << "You are eligible to vote. " << endl;
        cout << "Please proceed to the voting booth. " << endl;
        }
    else
        {
        cout << "You must register to vote. " << endl;
        cout << "Please fill out a registration form. " << endl;
        }
    }
else
    {
    cout << "You are too young to vote. " << endl;
    cout << "Thank you for your interest in voting. " << endl;
    }
```

Lesson 12.3 Logical Operators

Logical operators (also known as Boolean Operators) allow us to make multiple comparisons. We will examine three types of Logical operators, the and operator (&&), the or operator (||) and the not operator (!).

The and operator (&&) looks at two expressions and if they are both true it results in a true. If either or both are false the entire expression is false. Below is a table to help explain this.

Expression 1	Expression 2	Result
TRUE	TRUE	TRUE
TRUE	FALSE	FALSE
FALSE	TRUE	FALSE
FALSE	FALSE	FALSE

Now, let's put expressions into the table to illustrate how it works.

Expression 1	Expression 2	Result
5 > 2	3 < 6	TRUE
4 == 4	5 <= 2	FALSE
5 == 7	3 <= 7	FALSE
4 == 6	10 > 10	FALSE

In summary, the and operator results in a true only when both of the expressions are true. Any other combination where one or both expressions are false results in a false. So, use the and operator when you want to execute code only if both expressions are true.

USE LOGICAL AND OPERATOR INSTEAD OF NESTED IF STATEMENTS

```
int age = 0;
char registered = 'Y';
cout << "Enter your age:   ";
cin >> age;
cout << "Are you registered to vote Y or N:   ";
cin >> registered;
if (age >= 18 && registered == 'Y')
      {
              cout << "You are eligible to vote. " << endl;
              cout << "Please proceed to the voting booth. " << endl;
              }
      else
              {
              cout << "You are not eligible to vote. " << endl;
              cout << "Thank you for your interest in voting. " << endl;
              }
      return 0;
```

The or operator (||) looks at two expressions and if either expression or both are true it results in a true. If both are false the entire expression is false. Below is a table to help explain this.

Expression 1	Expression 2	Result
TRUE	TRUE	TRUE
TRUE	FALSE	TRUE
FALSE	TRUE	TRUE
FALSE	FALSE	FALSE

Now, let's put expressions into the table to illustrate how it works.

Expression 1	Expression 2	Result
5 > 2	3 > 6	TRUE
4 == 4	5 <= 2	TRUE
5 == 7	3 <= 3	TRUE
4 == 6	10 < 100	FALSE

In summary, the or operator results in a true when either or both of the expressions are true. Only when both expressions are false it results in a false. So, use the or operator when you want to execute code only if one or both expressions are true.

USE LOGICAL OR OPERATOR INSTEAD OF NESTED IF STATEMENTS

```
        int num1 = 0;
        int num2 = 0;

        cout << "Enter a number between 0 and 9:   ";
        cin >> num1;
        cout << "Enter a number between 0 and 9:   ";
        cin >> num2;

        if (num1 >= num2)|| num1 == num2)
            {
                    cout << num1 << " - " << num2 << " = " << num1 - num2 << endl;
            }
            else
            {
                    cout << num2 << " - " << num1 << " = " << num2 - num1 << endl;
            }
        return 0;
```

The above code examines two numbers the user entered and if the first number is greater than or equal to the second number, we can subtract the second number from the first number. Otherwise, we have to subtract the first number from the larger second number.

The not operator (!) is used to reverse the result of a comparison. Turning a true into a false or vice versa. We will look at an example of how we would use this in code:

```
        int num1 = 10
        int num2 = 10

        if !(num1 == num2)
            cout << "The result when num1 is not equal to num2" << endl;
        else
            cout << "The result when num1 is equal to num2" << endl;
```

Lesson 12.4 Sample Program

A sample C++ program is shown below. We have modified the code from the last lesson with the concepts we have learned in this lesson. We will use the If...Else statement to calculate deductions for married and dependent children. The current tax code allows a $10 exemption for those who are not married. If an employee is married they get a $16 exemption plus a $12 exemption for each dependent.

Input file for example: *40.0 10.00 2 Y John Dough*

```cpp
// pay1.cpp
// Date:
// Author:
#include <iostream>
#include <iomanip>
#include <string>
#include <fstream>

using namespace std;
int main()
{
    // declare variables
    double hoursWorked = 0.0;
    double rateOfPay = 0.00;
    double grossPay = 0.0;
    string name;
    double fedTax = 0.0;
    double netPay = 0.0;
    char married = 'Y';
    int dep = 0;
    double deduct = 0.0;

    // declare input and output file streams
    ifstream inFile;
    ofstream outFile;

    // open the files for input and output
    inFile.open("payin.txt");
    outFile.open("payroll.dat");

    // set format manipulators
    cout << fixed << showpoint;
    cout << setprecision(2);

    // get input data from payin.txt

    inFile >> hoursWorked;

    inFile >> rateOfPay;

    inFile >> dep;

    inFile >> married;

    getline(inFile, name);

    // processing statements
    grossPay = hoursWorked * rateOfPay;

    // use nested if to determine deductions
    if (married = 'Y')
        {
          if (dep > 0)
              {
              deduct = 16;
              deduct = deduct + (12 * dep);
              grossPay = grossPay - deduct;
```

```
            }
        else
            {
            deduct = 10;
            grossPay = grossPay - deduct;
            }
        }
    else
        {
        deduct = 10;
        grossPay = grossPay - deduct;
        }

    // decide how much federal tax the employee should pay
    // next 4 lines: demonstrate the single sided if statement
    if (grossPay <= 400.00)
        fedTax = grossPay * .12;
    if (grossPay > 400.00)
        fedTax = grossPay * .18;
    // calculate the net pay
    netPay = grossPay - fedTax - deduct;

    // display the result
    outFile << "Weekly Pay for: " << setw(6) << name << endl;
    outFile << "Gross Pay:      " << setw(6) << grossPay << endl;
    outFile << "Hours Worked:   " << setw(6) << hoursWorked << endl;
    outFile << "Rate of Pay:    " << setw(6) << rateOfPay << endl;
    outFile << "Married:        " << setw(6) << married << endl;
    outFile << "Dependents:     " << setw(6) << dep << endl;
    outFile << "Deductions:     " << setw(6) << deduct << endl;
    outFile << "Federal Tax:    " << setw(6) << fedTax << endl;
    outFile << "Net Pay:        " << setw(6) << netPay << endl;

inFile.close();
    outFile.close();
    return 0;
}       // End of Main Function
```

The output of this program will be in C:\payroll.dat and look like this:

```
Weekly pay for: John Dough
Gross Pay:      400.00
Hours Worked:    40.00
Rate of Pay:     10.00
Married:             Y
Dependents:          2
Deductions:      40.00
Federal Tax:     43.20
Net Pay:        356.80
```

Lesson 12.5 Summary

Unlike the simple, one-sided if statement, the if...else statement executes one block of statements if the expression evaluates to true and a different set of instructions if the expression evaluates to false.

Often a series of evaluations need to be done. This is called a nested if. If a first evaluation evaluates to true a second evaluation may be needed. Perhaps even a third or more evaluations may be done before an action is taken. Nesting may take place either side of the else statement.

The programmer can employ logical operators to extend the evaluation of the expression to evaluate multiple expressions in a single if structure. This requires using one of the Logical Operators, like the logical and, the logical or and the logical not operators.

End of Lesson Quiz

A if statement within another if statement block is called a _____ if statement.

When there are one set of statements to be executed when a condition evaluates to true and a second set of statements when the condition evaluates to false, you use the _____ _____ statement.

The && (and) operator and the || (or) operator are referred to as _____ operators.

Lesson 13
Decisions - Switch Statement

Objectives:
- Explain uses of the switch statement.
- Use the switch statement in a program.
- Compare the switch statement to nested if statements.
- Describe the break statement.

Lesson 13.1 SWITCH STATEMENT

Using nested if structures to test a variable for many possible values can make the program structure hard to understand and to debug. This is where we use the switch statement.

```
SYNTAX:
    switch(integer expression)
    {
        case constant-expression:
            // one or more true statements here
            break;
        case constant-expression:
            // one or more true statements here
            break;
        *
            repeat as many times as necessary
        *
        default:
            // one or more default statements here
    }  // end of switch statement
```

A switch statement allows for as many comparisons to an integer expression as necessary to test all possible conditions. The default at the end will be executed only if none of the other conditions are met.

For Example, we have a menu which allows us to choose from selections 0 thru 3. Any other value receives a message that an invalid value was entered. First we look at the problem solved with an if statement. The look at the same problem solved with a switch statement.

```
IF EXAMPLE:
    int response;
    cout << "Main Menu" << endl;
    cout << " 1  Program #1" << endl;
    cout << " 2  Program #2" << endl;
    cout << " 3  Program #3" << endl;
    cout << "Make Your Selection: ";
    cin >> response;
    if (response == 1)
        cout << "Program 1 Selected" << endl;
    else if (response == 2)
        cout << "Program 2 Selected" << endl;
    else if (response == 3)
        cout << "Program 3 Selected" << endl;
    else
        cout << "Invalid code entered" << endl;
```

```
SWITCH EXAMPLE:
     int response;
     cout << "Main Menu" << endl;
     cout << " 1   Program #1" << endl;
     cout << " 2   Program #2" << endl;
     cout << " 3   Program #3" << endl;
     cout << "Make Your Selection: ";
     cin >> response;

         switch(response)
         {
           case 1:
               cout << "Program 1 Selected" << endl;
               break;
           case 2:
               cout << "Program 2 Selected" << endl;
               break;
           case 3:
               cout << "Program 3 Selected" << endl;
               break;
           default:
               cout << "Invalid code entered" << endl;
         }   // end of switch statement
```

The variable passed as an argument to the switch() statement is compared with the value in each case statement and the instruction(s) following the colon (:) are executed. If there is not a matching case statement, the default statement provides statement(s) to be executed. Note that each case statement block contains a break; statement. This causes the program to transfer control to the first statement after the bracket at the end of the switch code block structure.

The variable examined must be an int or a char data type. You may test for ranges of numbers or assign more than one case to a code block.

```
     EXAMPLE:
     char response;
     cout << "Enter a letter A thru D in either upper or lower case: ";
     cin >> response;
     switch(response)
     {
       case 'a':
         case 'A':
           cout << "Option A Selected" << endl;
           break;
       case 'b':
         case 'B':
           cout << "Option B Selected" << endl;
           break;
       case 'c':
         case 'C':
           cout << "Option C Selected" << endl;
           break;
       case 'd':
         case 'D':
           cout << "Option D Selected" << endl;
           break;
       default:
           cout << "Invalid code entered" << endl;
     }        // end of switch statement
```

In the example the user enters a response to the prompt which is stored in a variable named response. Since the program allows the entry of upper or lowercase letters we need to treat upper case A the same as lower case a. We do this by allowing the comparison of both upper case and lower case letters and if either match the contents of the variable response we execute the same instruction block. If the user enters a code not specifically coded into the switch statement, the statements following default at the end of the structure are executed. If the default is omitted, the instruction immediately following the end of the switch structure is executed.

At the end of each case, the break statement is executed. This statement directs the processing to the instruction immediately following the switch statement block. Once the condition has been found and executed you need to exit the switch structure to eliminate the possibility of any more processing. Not including the break statement may result in the default condition being executed and this may cause errors in the output of the program.

Another example of the switch structure:

```
EXAMPLE:
    int main()
    {
        int num1;
        cout << "Enter a number between 1 and 5: ";
        cin num1;
        cout << "The number you entered is: << num1 << endl;
        switch (num1)
        {
        case 0:
            cout << "Zero Not within acceptable range." << endl;
            break;
        case 1:
            cout << "You entered the number one. " << endl;
            break;
        case 2:
        case 3:
        case 4:
            cout << "You entered a 2, 3, or 4." << endl;
            break;
        case 5:
            cout << "You entered a five." << endl;
            break;
        default:
            cout << "Not within acceptable range. " << endl;
        }
        cout << "This message is outside the switch statement." << endl;
        return 0;
    } // end of main function
```

This switch statement only accepts values 1 through 5. Any other value returns a message that the number entered was not in an acceptable range. Note the third case statement. This evaluates a range of numbers and if the number is in that range returns a message.

Lesson 13.2 Sample Program

A sample C++ program is shown below. We have modified the code from the last lesson with the concepts we have learned in this lesson. This lesson featured the switch statement. We will use the switch statement to determine the cost of the health package selected by the employee and deduct it from the gross pay before taxes. Package 1 costs $18 per pay; package 2 costs $22 per pay; package 3 costs $28 per pay and package 4 costs $33 per pay.

Input file for example: `40.0 10.00 2 Y 3 John Dough`

```cpp
// pay1.cpp
// Date:
// Author:
#include <iostream>
#include <iomanip>
#include <string>
#include <fstream>

using namespace std;
int main()
{
    // declare variables
    double hoursWorked = 0.0;
    double rateOfPay = 0.00;
    double grossPay = 0.0;
    string name;
    double fedTax = 0.0;
    double netPay = 0.0;
    char married = 'Y';
    int dep = 0;
    double deduct = 0.0;
    int health = 0;
    double price = 0.0;

    // declare input and output file streams
    ifstream inFile;
    ofstream outFile;

    // open the files for input and output
    inFile.open("payin.txt");
    outFile.open("payroll.dat");

    // set format manipulators
    cout << fixed << showpoint;
    cout << setprecision(2);

    // get input data from payin.txt

    inFile >> hoursWorked;
    inFile >> rateOfPay;
    inFile >> dep;
    inFile >> married;
    inFile >> health;
    getline(inFile, name);

    // processing statements
    grossPay = hoursWorked * rateOfPay;

    // use nested if to determine deductions
    if (married = 'Y')
        {
          if (dep > 0)
              {
              deduct = 16;
```

```cpp
            deduct = deduct + (12 * dep);
            grossPay = grossPay - deduct;
            }
        else
            {
            deduct = 16;
            grossPay = grossPay - deduct;
            }
        }
  else
      {
      deduct = 10;
      grossPay = grossPay - deduct;
      }

// determine the cost of the health package selected.
// this is a pretax deduction
switch(health)
    {
    case 0:
        grossPay = grossPay - 0;
        price = 0.0;
        break;
    case 1:
        grossPay = grossPay - 18.00;
        price = 18.00;
        break;
    case 2:
        grossPay = grossPay - 22.00;
        price = 22.00;
        break;
    case 3:
        grossPay = grossPay - 28.00;
        price = 28.00;
        break;
    case 4:
        grossPay = grossPay - 33.00;
        price = 33.00;
        break;
    default:
        grossPay = grossPay - 0;
        price = 0.0;
    }  // end of switch statement

// decide how much federal tax the employee should pay
// next 4 lines: demonstrate the single sided if statement
if (grossPay <= 400.00)
    fedTax = grossPay * .12;
if (grossPay > 400.00)
    fedTax = grossPay * .18;

// calculate the net pay
netPay = grossPay - fedTax - deduct;

// display the result
outFile << "Weekly Pay for: " << setw(6) << name << endl;
outFile << "Gross Pay:      " << setw(6) << grossPay << endl;
outFile << "Hours Worked:   " << setw(6) << hoursWorked << endl;
outFile << "Rate of Pay:    " << setw(6) << rateOfPay << endl;
```

```
        outFile << "Married:        " << setw(6) << married << endl;
        outFile << "Dependents:     " << setw(6) << dep << endl;
        outFile << "Deductions:     " << setw(6) << deduct << endl;
        outFile << "Health:         " << setw(6) << price << endl;
        outFile << "Federal Tax:    " << setw(6) << fedTax << endl;
        outFile << "Net Pay:        " << setw(6) << netPay << endl;

    inFile.close();
    outFile.close();
    return 0;
}  // End of Main Function
```

The output of this program will be in C:\payroll.dat and look like this:

```
    Weekly pay for: John Dough
    Gross Pay:      400.00
    Hours Worked:    40.00
    Rate of Pay:     10.00
    Married:             Y
    Dependents:          2
    Deductions:      40.00
    Health:          28.00
    Federal Tax:     39.84
    Net Pay:        360.16
```

Lesson 13.3 Summary

The last, and probably the least understood of the decision statements is the switch statement. This is used when a variable (or expression) must be tested for many different values and each needs to be treated individually. Each case statement must end in a colon and the last statement to be executed for each case must be a break statement. If none of the conditions are met, a default statement may be executed if present. If not present, the program continues with the next statement after the switch block.

End of Lesson Quiz

The _____ statement allows for as many comparisons to an integer expression as necessary to test all possible conditions.

If there is not a matching case statement, the _____ statement provides statement(s) to be executed.

The variable examined in a switch statement must be an _____ or _____ data type.

At the end of each case statement block, there must be a _____ statement.

SECTION IV - Repetition Structure

Lesson 14 - For Loop

Lesson 15 - While Loop and Do Loop

Lesson 16 - Nested Loops

Lesson 14
Repetition Structure - For Loop

Objectives:
- Explain the repetition structure.
- Use the For loop structure in a program.
- Explain ending values of the counter after the loop executes.
- Compare and contrast the increment vs decrement loop structures.

Lesson 14.1 REPETITION STRUCTURE

The repetition structure allows the programmer to create programs that will do groups of instructions repeatedly until a predefined condition stops the process, the program stops the process or the process runs out of data. There are several different types of loops and in this lesson we will discuss the For Loop structure.

Lesson 14.2 FOR LOOP

The For statement creates a counter controlled loop. Simply, this means that the program specifies how many times the loop will be executed. The program can determine how many times the loop is to be executed before entering the loop. The syntax of the For Loop includes determining a starting point, determining an end point and optionally the increment or decrement that will be applied to the starting point at the end of each execution of the loop. The syntax looks like this:

```
for (initialization; test-expression; increment)
    {
            statements to be executed
    }
```

The sequence of operations for the typical for loop is as follows:

1. use the initialization to determine the starting counter.
2. compare the starting counter to the test expression and if true do the statements to be executed. If false, go to the statement following the ending curly brace. This exits the loop.
3. increment or decrement the counter based on the value given (if no increment is specified, add one)
4. go to step 2

Let's create a small for loop that prints "1, 2, 3" on the screen. We need to build a loop that starts with a counter equal to 1 and stops when that counter reaches 3 and displays the contents of the counter on the screen, each number separated by a comma and a space

```
EXAMPLE:
        for (i=1; i<=3; i++)
            {
            cout << i << ", ";
            }
        cout << "End of Program" << endl;
```

1. initialize the counter named i to 1.

2. continue to do the loop statement(s) as long as the contents of i are less than or equal to 3.
3. set the increment value to 1.
4. if the contents of i are less than or equal to 3 go to step 5 otherwise go to step 8.
5. display the contents of i followed by a comma and a space on the common output.
6. increment the contents of i by the increment value 1.
7. go to step 4.
8. execute the next statement after the closing curley brace (}).

Practice this loop on paper and note the value of i after the loop ends. Is this value what you expected the loop to end at?

We can also use the for loop to start at a higher number and count down by decrementing the counter each time through the loop. In the next sample we will reverse the last example and display "3, 2, 1" on the common output.

EXAMPLE:

```
            for (i=3; i<=1; i--)
                {
                cout << i << ", ";
                }
            cout << "End of Program" << endl;
```

1. initialize the counter named i to 3.
2. continue to do the loop statement(s) as long as the contents of i are less than or equal to 1.
3. set the increment value to -1 (decrement).
4. if the contents of i are less than or equal to 1 go to step 5 otherwise go to step 8.
5. display the contents of i followed by a comma and a space on the common output.
6. decrement the contents of i by 1.
7. go to step 4.
8. next statement after the closing curley brace (}).

Practice this loop on paper and note the value of i after the loop ends. Is this value what you expected the loop to end at?

Lesson 14.3 Sample Program

We now need a sample program to show the For loop statement as it would be used in a computer program. Since it is a counter loop we need to construct a program that executes some statements a number of times. Professor Smith needs a program to enter grades for his Computer Technology classes to calculate a final grade. Since each class has a different number of grades he would like to enter the number of grades to be entered and have the program ask him at the beginning how many grades he needs to enter. Then when all the grades have been entered he would like the program to average these grades and display the average grade on the common ouput device.

Test data to enter at the prompts to test the program:

```
        Enter number of students:  4
        Enter grade number 1:  89
        Enter grade number 2:  94
        Enter grade number 3:  76
        Enter grade number 4:  92
```

```cpp
// grades.cpp
// Date:
// Author:

#include <iostream>
#include <iomanip>

using namespace std;
int main()
{
    // declare variables
    double sumgrades = 0.0;
    double grades = 0.0;
    double avggrade = 0.0;
    int count = 0;
    int i;

    // set format manipulators
    cout << fixed << showpoint;
    cout << setprecision(1);

    // Enter number of students in the class
    cout << "Enter number of students: ";
    cin >> count;

    for (i = 0; i < count; i++)
    {
        cout << "Enter grade number " << i << " : ";
        cin >> grade;
        sumgrades += grade;
    }

    // calculate the average and display
    avggrade = sumgrades / count;
    cout << "Number of Grades: " << setw(6);
    cout << setfill(' ') << count << endl;
    cout << "Sum of Grades: " << setw(7);
    cout << setfill(' ') << sumgrades << endl;
    cout << "Average of Grades: " << setw(4);
    cout << setfill(' ') << avggrade << endl;

    return 0;
}        // end of main function
```

The output of this program should look like this:

```
Average of Grades for Prof. Smith's Class
Number of Grades:      4
Sum of Grades:       351
Average of Grades:    87.8
```

Lesson 14.4 Summary

Repeating groups of instructions is one of the most powerful feature of any programming language. This is where the program exploits the true power of the computer. The For loop is a counter controlled that is used to execute a loop a predetermined number of times unless prematurely exited prior to completion. The instruction sets a beginning value, a condition to end the loop and a value to increment (or decrement) the counter each time through the statement block that makes up the loop instructions.

End of Lesson Quiz

The _____ structure allows the programmer to create programs that will do groups of instructions repeatedly.

The _____ loop statement creates a counter controlled loop.

Lesson 15
Repetition Structure - While Loop and Do While Loop

Objectives:

- Explain the repetition structure.
- Use the While loop structure in a program.
- Use the do while loop structure in a program..
- Compare and contrast the while and do while loop structures.

Lesson 15.1 REPETITION STRUCTURE

The repetition structure allows the programmer to create programs that will do groups of instructions repeatedly until the process is stopped by the evaluation of an expression. This may be caused by examining a variable, testing for the end of a file, or based on the user entering a value that, when tested, stops the program. Our programs up to this point have been able to process one set of data and then to do a second set we would have to restart the program. This is fine to do one or two sets of data but would be a real disaster to have to do this for hundreds or even thousands of sets of data.

A good example is the payroll example. To run the program repeatedly for each of five employees would be no big deal. However, for a company with five thousand employees, this would be as tedious as doing the payroll by hand. So, there has to be a better way. The better way is the repetition structure.

The repetition structure is also used to process sequential data files. Sequential data files often contain hundreds or even thousands of data records. The proper repetition structure will go through the file, one record at a time and process each record according to the rules set up by the program and when the file has been completely processed, end the processing.

Now, let's take a look at the various repetition structures available in C++.

Lesson 15.2 WHILE LOOP

We can use the while loop (repetition) structure to repeat groups of instructions. The instruction does a block of statements WHILE an expression is true. When the expression tests false the execution of the program continues with the statement immediately following the statement block for the WHILE statement. The syntax for these are similar:

```
while (expression)
    {
        statements to be executed while
        expression evaluates true
    }  // end of while
```

Note the expression must be contained within parenthesis and you may have multiple expressions joined by logical operators. Secondly note there is NO SEMICOLON after the while expression. If a semicolon is present the condition is evaluated and then all the statements in the statement block will NOT be executed regardless if the condition evaluated true or false. Third, the rules regarding the expression and its evaluation are exactly like the rules of evaluation we studied in the Selection Structure. Lastly, the statement block must be surrounded by curly braces. All statements in the statement block must end in a semicolon.

The WHILE statement is called a PRETEST loop since the expression is evaluated prior to doing any of the statements in the statement block. Therefore, based on the evaluation the statements in the statement block may or may not be executed. In the EXAMPLE below we have a loop that will continue while the variable counter has a value that is less than or equal to 3. Also, note that in the loop statements there is an instruction that increments the value in counter by one. If we did not provide some way to change the value of counter in the loop to eventually make the evaluation expression false, we would have an "infinite loop". This condition may look like the computer "locked up" or data may scroll across the screen and never stop.

EXAMPLE:

```
        int counter = 1;
        while (counter <= 3)
              {
                    cout << counter << ", ";
                    counter++;
              }  // end of while
```

OR:

```
        while (!eof)
              {
                    infile >> name;
                    infile >> address;
              }  // end of while
```

The first example executes a loop until the counter becomes greater than 3. Note that in the loop the counter is incremented by one each time through the instructions. The second example continues to execute the loop while there is information in the input file specified by the program. When the input file runs out of data, the loop ceases to execute.

Lesson 15.3 DO...WHILE LOOP

The WHILE loop is a pretest loop, meaning that the expression is evaluated before any loop instructions are executed and if the expression test to false, the loop statements will not be executed. On the other hand, the Do..While loop is a POSTTEST loop. In a post test loop, the statements in the loop will be executed at least once, because, the evaluation is at the end of the loop. As in the While loop, make sure there is an instruction in the loop that alters the variable evaluated in the while expression to insure that at some point the expression will evaluate to false so we do not wind up with an "infinite loop".

```
        do
              {
                    statements to be executed while
                    the expression is true;
              }
        while (expression);
```

Note in the syntax, the last line (the while statement) where the expression is evaluated, that line ends with a semicolon (;). Failure to include this will result in a syntax error. Let's look at an example of the code required to start counting at 3 and decrement by one until and produce output on the common output like this: "3, 2, 1"

EXAMPLE:

```
        int counter = 3;
        do
              {
                    cout << counter << ", ";
                    counter--;
              }
```

```
        while (counter <= 1);
        cout << "After the loop the counter is: " << counter << endl;
```

Lesson 15.4 Sentinel Controlled Loop

If you don't know how many times a loop needs to be executed your expression in the while statement will need to evaluate the contents of a variable for a signal to end the loop. Here is a sample program to illustrate Sentinel Controlled loops. First there is a priming read that instructs the user to enter a temperature or 999 to exit (999 is the sentinel, a value outside the normal values that will be entered). Then the loop begins by evaluating what was entered. This gives the opportunity to allow the user to enter 999 to exit before starting the process. Any other value enters the loop statements. The temp entered is accumulated in the variable called totaltemp. The counter variable keeps count of how many temperatures have been entered. Lastly the operator is instructed to enter the next temperature or 999 to quit the loop and calculate the average. This second read is inside the loop structure.

```
EXAMPLE:
    #include<iostream>
    using namespace std;

    int main()
    {
        // declare variables
        double temp = 0.0;
        double totaltemp = 0.0; // accumulator
        double avgtemp = 0.0;
        int counter = 0;  // counter
        // priming read
        cout << "Enter Temperature, 999 to quit";
        cin >> temp;
        // while loop ends when operator enters 999
        while (temp != 999)
        {
            totaltemp = totaltemp + temp;
            counter++;
            // operator determines when loop ends
            // or enters another temp value.
            cout << "Enter Temperature, 999 to quit";
            cin >> temp;
        }
        // when complete, calcualate average temp.
        avgtemp = totaltemp / counter;
        // display the result
        cout << "Average Temperature: " << avgtemp << endl;
        return 0;
    }      // end of main function
```

The sentinel value 999 was used because it is a value that would never be a valid temperature. Actually you could use any value (positive or negative) as a sentinel. In our example we could have used a (-555 or 678 or -987) as sentinel values. Any number that would indicate invalid input.

Lesson 15.5 Flag Controlled Loop

A flag controlled loop uses a bool variable to control the loop. The while loop evaluates the variable and when it evaluates to true the loop exits.

```
    bool found = false;
    int counter = 0;

    while (!found)      // not found is true
    {
          cout << "Loop Statement " << counter << endl;
          if (counter == 3)
                { found = true;}
          else
                {counter = counter + 1;}
    }  // end of while
```

Note that within the loop statement block there is a statement that changes the bool variable named found, from FALSE to TRUE, so when the counter contains a 3 the loop is terminated.

Lesson 15.6 EOF Controlled Loop

When obtaining input from a file, most often you cannot know exactly how many records you will be reading. This situation calls for an EOF (End Of File) controlled loop. This loop will exit when the program attempts to read after reading the last record of the file.

There are a couple of ways to write a counter controlled loop. Here are some examples of the two different ways to write the loop.

```
Example 1:
    double accountnumber = 0.0;
    int amount = 0;

    inFile >> accountnumber >> amount;

    while (inFile)
    {
          cout << "Account Number: " << accountnumber << endl;
          cout << "Amount        : " << amount << endl;
          inFile >> accountnumber >> amount;
    }   // end of while

Example 2:
    double accountnumber = 0.0;
    int amount = 0;

    inFile >> accountnumber >> amount;

    while (!eof)
    {
          cout << "Account Number: " << accountnumber << endl;
          cout << "Amount        : " << amount << endl;
          inFile >> accountnumber >> amount;
    }   // end of while
```

In both examples the condition that causes the program to exit the loop is when the end-of-file is reached on the file.

Lesson 15.7 Sample Program

A sample C++ program is shown below. Here is a program that demonstrates the While loop (pretest).

```cpp
// pay1.cpp
// Date:
// Author:
#include <iostream>
#include <iomanip>
#include <string>
#include <fstream>

using namespace std;
int main()
{
    // declare variables
    double hoursWorked = 0.0;
    double rateOfPay = 0.00;
    double grossPay = 0.0;
    string name;
    double fedTax = 0.0;
    double netPay = 0.0;
    char married = 'Y';
    int dep = 0;
    double deduct = 0.0;
    int health = 0;
    double price = 0.0;
    double depded = 0.0;
    int i;

    // declare input and output file streams
    ifstream inFile;
    ofstream outFile;

    // open the files for input and output
    inFile.open("payin.txt");
    outFile.open("payroll.dat");

    // set format manipulators
    cout << fixed << showpoint;
    cout << setprecision(2);

    // get input data from payin.txt
    // priming reads
    inFile >> hoursWorked;
    inFile >> rateOfPay;
    inFile >> dep;
    inFile >> married;
    inFile >> health;
    getline(inFile, name);

    // Start Processing Loop
    while (inFile)
    {
    // processing statements
    grossPay = hoursWorked * rateOfPay;

    // use nested if to determine deductions
    if (married = 'Y')
        {
         deduct = 16;
         grossPay = grossPay - deduct;
```

```
        }
    else
        {
        deduct = 8;
        grossPay = grossPay - deduct;
        }

// Deductions for dependents
depded = 0.0;
for (i = 1; i <= dep; i++)
    {
        depded = depded + 12.00;
    }

// determine the cost of the health package selected.
// this is a pretax deduction
switch(health)
    {
    case 0:
        grossPay = grossPay - 0;
        price = 0.0;
        break;
    case 1:
        grossPay = grossPay - 18.00;
        price = 18.00;
        break;
    case 2:
        grossPay = grossPay - 22.00;
        price = 22.00;
        break;
    case 3:
        grossPay = grossPay - 28.00;
        price = 28.00;
        break;
    case 4:
        grossPay = grossPay - 33.00;
        price = 33.00;
        break;
    default:
        grossPay = grossPay - 0;
        price = 0.0;
    }   // end of switch statement
// decide how much federal tax the employee should pay
// next 4 lines: demonstrate the single sided if statement
if (grossPay <= 400.00)
    fedTax = grossPay * .12;
if (grossPay > 400.00)
    fedTax = grossPay * .18;

// calculate the net pay
netPay = grossPay - fedTax - deduct;

// display the result
outFile << "Weekly Pay for: " << setw(6) << name << endl;
outFile << "Gross Pay:      " << setw(6) << grossPay << endl;
outFile << "Hours Worked:   " << setw(6) << hoursWorked << endl;
outFile << "Rate of Pay:    " << setw(6) << rateOfPay << endl;
outFile << "Married:        " << setw(6) << married << endl;
outFile << "Dependents:     " << setw(6) << dep << endl;
```

```
outFile << "Deductions:      " << setw(6) << deduct + depded << endl;
outFile << "Health:          " << setw(6) << price << endl;
outFile << "Federal Tax:     " << setw(6) << fedTax << endl;
outFile << "Net Pay:         " << setw(6) << netPay << endl;

// Read Next Record from the input file
// get input data from payin.txt
inFile >> hoursWorked;
inFile >> rateOfPay;
inFile >> dep;
inFile >> married;
inFile >> health;
getline(inFile, name);

} // End of While loop

inFile.close();
outFile.close();
return 0;
}       // End of Main Function
```

The input to the program for testing:

Hours	RateOfPay	Dependent	Married	Health	Name
40.00	10.00	2.00	0	28.00	John Dough
37.50	22.00	3.00	0	53.00	Sam Spade
55.00	8.50	0.00	0	22.00	Don Knott

The output of this program will be in C:\payroll.dat contain 3 records each record formatted like record one shown below:

```
Weekly pay for: John Dough
Gross Pay:      400.00
Hours Worked:    40.00
Rate of Pay:     10.00
Married:             Y
Dependents:          2
Deductions:      40.00
Health:          28.00
Federal Tax:     39.84
Net Pay:        360.16
```

Lesson 15.8 Summary

The repetition structures we just reviewed are the While loop and the Do While loop. The first is a pretest loop and the second a post test loop. It is important that within the statement block for both types of loops, that the condition that they test to exit the loop be changed. Failure to do so will result in an "infinite loop" or a situation where the loop never completes so the program never completes. The while loop (the pretest loop) may never execute. This is true when the program arrives at the evaluation at the beginning of the loop and evaluates to false. The code in the statement block never gets executed. This is not the situation with the Do While loop. This post test loop will always execute the code in the statement block at least once. So, when choosing which type of loop to use, consider the implications of always executing the code with perhaps never executing the code.

These loops may be controlled by a counter, a sentinel, a flag, or the end of file condition when reading a file. Regardless of the type of control it is necessary that somewhere within the loop the control factor will eventually take the program out of the statement block.

End of Lesson Quiz

Data files often contain hundreds or even thousands of data records, the _____ structure makes processing this volume of data much easier.

The _____ loop does a block of statements as long as the evaluation condition evaluates to true.

The While statement is a _____ loop since the expression is evaluated before doing any statements in the statement block.

The Do...While loop is a _____ loop as the statement block is executed once, before any evaluation of the loop condition.

Lesson 16
Repetition Structure - Nested Loops

Objectives:

- Explain uses of nested loops.
- Use nested loops.
- Use the break statement.
- Use the continue statement.

Lesson 16.1 NESTED LOOPS

Sometimes it is necessary to put one loop inside another loop. This is referred to as a "nested" loop. We will look at an example where we will build a triangle out of asterisks (*). We can make this triangle out of a fixed number of asterisks across a fixed number of lines with the following code.

```cpp
#include<iostream>
using namespace std;
int main()
{
//declare variables
int i = 0;
int j = 0;

//set up outer loop - determines number of rows (max. 5)
for (i=1; i<=5; i++)
    {
    // set up inner loop - determines number of * (max. 5)
    for (j=1; j<=i; j++)
    {
        cout << "*";
    }
    cout << endl;
    }

return 0;
}    // end of main function
```

OUTPUT:

```
*
* *
* * *
* * * *
* * * * *
```

The "outer" loop controls the number of lines. This loop will be executed five times so we expect to get five lines. The "inner" loop determines the number of asterisks on each line. It will put one asterisk at a time on the line. The number of asterisks will be equal to the line number being processed. Therefore there will be one asterisk on line one, two on line two, and so on, up to five on line five.

We can nest all types of repetition and decision structures. Below we have an example of a For loop nested in a While loop and in the lesson on break and continue we have a decision structure nested in a repetition structure. The program reads a file with a row number and the number of seats in that row. The while loop reads the file and puts the start of the output line. The for loop procuces a # sign for each seat in the row.

EXAMPLE:

```
inFile >> rownumber >> seats;

while (inFile)  // outer loop
{
      cout << "Row " << rownumber << " ";
      for (i = 0; i < seats; i++)    // inner loop
      {
            cout << "#";
      }
      cout << endl;
      inFile >> rownumber >> seats;
}  // end of while
```

Below is a sample of the input to this loop and a sample of the resulting output.

SAMPLE INPUT:
```
         1 8
         2 10
         3 10
         4 10
```

SAMPLE OUTPUT:
```
         Row 1 ########
         Row 2 ##########
         Row 3 ##########
         Row 4 ##########
```

The first row has 8 seats (represented by 8 #) in the row. Rows 2, 3, and 4 all have 10 seats (represented by 10 #) in each row. This pattern corresponds to the values input for each row.

Lesson 16.2 BREAK and CONTINUE STATEMENTS

When we coded the switch statement we used the BREAK statement to exit the structure when we found a match. The break statement can be used to break out of any of the decision or repetition structures before they complete. Let's look at an example where we break out of a while loop prematurely.

EXAMPLE:

```
inFile >> accountnumber >> amount;

while (inFile)
{
      if (accountnumber > 5555)
      {
            break;    // invalid account number
      }
      else
```

```
        {
                totalamount = totalamount + amount;
        {
            inFile >> accountnumber >> amount;
    }    // end of while
```

The CONTINUE statement allows you to break the execution of the loop statements and return to the evaluation expression at the start of the loop. Consider the problem where you are taking in numbers but if a negative number is encountered you want to skip that number.

EXAMPLE:

```
    int total = 0;
    int num = 0;
    cin >> num;
    while (cin)
    {
        if (num < 0)
        {
                cout << "Negative number not permitted" << endl;
                cin >> num;
                continue;
        }
        sum = sum + num;
        cin >> num;
    }   // end of while
```

If the user enters a negative number the test within the while loop for a value in num that is less than 0 (a negative number), the program accepts another number and then continues back to the while statement. Pressing enter without entering a value will terminate the program.

Lesson 16.3 Sample Program

A sample C++ program is shown below. For this week we are leaving the payroll example we are building and presenting a different code sample which will do a better job of illustrating the concepts learned in this section.

```
    // repetition.cpp
    // Date:
    // Author:
    #include <iostream>
    #include <iomanip>
    #include <string>
    #include <fstream>

    using namespace std;
    int main()
    {
        // declare variables
        int hours = 0;
        int minutes = 0;
        int seconds = 0;
        int x = 0;
        int y = 0;
        int z = 0;

        // hours loop
```

```
        for (x = 0; x <= 23; x++)
            {
              cout << "Hour: " << x << endl;
              // minutes loop
              for (y = 0; y <= 59; y++)
              {
                    cout << "    Minute: " << y << endl;
                    // seconds loop
                    for (z = 0; z <= 59; z++)
                    {
                          cout << "        Second: " << z << endl;
                    }
              }
            }

        return 0;
}     // End of Main Function
```

Lesson 16.4 Summary

As in decision structures we can nest repetition structures. We can nest decision structures within repetition structures and repetition structures within decision structures as well as repetition structures within other repetition structures. Each nesting adds to the complexity and it is even more important to remember to provide exit conditions for all loops.

The break statement allows the program to exit a loop before the conditions are satisfied. If using a loop to search for a record, it makes sense to exit the loop as soon as the record is found.

The continue statement sends the execution back to the evaluation portion of the loop without continuing processing the statements in the code block.

End of Lesson Quiz

Putting a loop within another loop is referred to as a _____ loop.

The _____ statement in a loop returns control to the start of the loop.

The _____ statement stops the execution of the loop statements and transfers control to the first statement after the end of the loop.

SECTION V - Functions

Lesson 17
Using Functions and Built-In Functions

Objectives:

- Define functions.
- Explain Uses of built-in functions.
- Use built-in functions.

Lesson 17.1 FUNCTIONS DEFINED

A function can be defined as a section of code that makes up a program or part of a program. A function is a complete unit of C++ code with a start and end point and its own set of variables. Every C++ program is at the minimum one function, the function we call main. When a C++ program begins it starts executing the main function. Subsequently, the main function may invoke other functions and those functions may invoke other functions. The syntax of a function is as follows:

```
functiontype    functionname(arguments)
{
      Function statements;
}  // end of function
```

The main function looks like this:

```
int   main()
{
      Main function statements;
      return 0;
}  // end of main function
```

The functiontype is either void or one of the datatypes like int, float, etc.. We will discuss the meaning of this later in this section.

Next is the functionname which is the name of the function. When selecting a name for your function you should use the same naming conventions as we discussed for variables. The name should describe the purpose of the function as well as the same naming rules as we established for variables in Section 2.

Then we have a set of parenthesis () and inside those parenthesis you may find a list of arguments (or parameters) to be passed from the calling function to the called function. In talking about functions we use the terms argument and parameter interchangeably. There may be a list of arguments or in some cases the parenthesis will be empty. An argument in the prototype and the function header (formal arguments) consists of a data type and a variable name. An argument in the function call (actual arguments) consists of a variable name, one that exists in the calling program.

The statements to be executed by the function are next and must be enclosed in a set of curly braces {}. If the function has a datatype of anything other than void it must have a return statement that returns a value of that datatype to the calling function. All of the programs in this course will have the main function return a zero (0).

Lesson 17.2 WHY USE FUNCTIONS

Functions are the basic building blocks for C++ programs. As we said earlier, all C++ programs consist of at least one function, that being the main function.

Functions are useful in that they allow the programmer to program tasks that may be used by more than one program one time in a separate container so they can be used by other programs. Write once, test once and then use the true and tested code many times.

Once a function has been programmed and tested it can be stored in a library to be used in other programs and reduce the development time by having code already written and tested. Functions are also useful in larger applications, to allow a large program to be broken into parts that can be distributed to a team of programmers. No that does not mean that if it takes a hundred hours for a programmer to write a program, one hundred programmers can write it in one hour. However, there are significant time benefits to breaking up large programs between a team of programmers.

In the examples and sample programming exercises in our course, it is difficult to see the benefits of functions. It is usually easier to complete the exercises without functions and all the extra work and bother that goes into developing a function. However, it is important for a C++ programmer to be proficient in functions. Understanding functions is also important in using other modern programming languages. Nearly all programming languages provide this functionality and it is used extensively. Understanding functions is key to understanding object oriented programming as well as programming in most modern programming languages.

For simplicity and the purposes of these programs we will always have the main function as the first function of any program. This is not a constraint of C++ but in the spirit of simplicity this is the way we will explain and use functions.

We will discuss two types of functions in this section. We will discuss Built-in Functions in this lesson, and two types of Programmer Defined Functions; (1) VOID Functions and (2) Value Returning Functions in future lessons.

Lesson 17.3 BUILT IN FUNCTIONS

We will start with Built-in Functions. These are functions that come with your C++ compiler. Most of these functions are exactly the same in every C++ compiler you will encounter. They are simply C++ programs, stored in libraries, that have been written and tested to do some common tasks. Two very common examples are the functions to take the square root of a number and the function to raise a number to a power. The function needs some information from the programmer (called arguments or parameters) and then when the function is executed, it takes that information, calculates the answer and provides the answer back to the calling program. These functions are usually value returning functions.

First we will examine the function that raises a number to a power. Example, what is 2 to the power of 3 ? The pow() function will do this calculation for us. The syntax of this function is:

```
returnvariable = pow(number, power):
```

This function requires two arguments, the number and the power. It does the calculation and stores the answer to the returnvariable. A function that returns a value (value returning function), must have a place to put the value it is returning.

In a program it may look something like this:

```
float answr = 0.0;
answr = pow(2, 3);
```

```
cout << answr;
```

A variable named answr of the datatype float is assigned and given the value of 0.0. The second line is where the function is called to do the calculation. The calculated result will be stored in the variable named answr. On the right of the assignment operator is the function pow(). Since pow requires two arguments, the number and the power we use the function with the arguments 2 and 3. At the completion of the statement the variable named answr will contain the number calculated (8). Then using the common output statement (cout) the result is displayed.

Let's write a little program that will calculate the answer:

```cpp
// cube.cpp
#include<iostream>
#include<cmath>
using namespace std;
void main()  {
     float numbr = (float) 2;
     float answr = (float) 0.0;

     answr = pow(numbr, 3);

     cout << "The Answer is:  " << answr;
}  // End of Main Function
```

Note that there are now two include directives at the top of the program. The function for the common mathematical functions is stored in a library named cmath (the library for the code used to calculate the pow() function). So when we use these mathematical functions we must tell the program to use the appropriate library of functions.

We assign two variables of type float because we can expect a number with a fraction as an answer. The first, named numbr is where we will store the value that will be raised to the power of three and the second, named answr is where the function will store the result when it returns the answer.

The next instruction is where the calculation occurs. The calling program receive the result of the calculation in the variable named answr. To the right of the assignment operator we find the built-in function with two arguments (or parameters). The name of the built-in function that the program will call, is pow and it is followed by two arguments in parenthesis. The first argument is the variable name numbr where we have stored the number we wish to raise to a power. The second argument is the numeric literal 3 which represents the power that the contents of the variable numbr will be raised to. When the function completes it will return a value and store it in the variable to the left of the assignment operator, answr.

The last statement in the program is where we output the answer. The string literal "The Answer is: " will be displayed on the screen followed by the contents of the variable named answr.

Here is an example of a program that uses the pow() function and asks the user for two different inputs, a number and a power, and returns the answer directly to a cout statement for output to the common output device.

```cpp
// cube.cpp
#include<iostream>
#include<cmath>
using namespace std;
void main()  {
     float numbr = (float) 0.0;
     int powr = 0;
```

```
        cout << "Enter a number: ";
        cin >> numbr;

        cout << "Enter a power: ";
        cin >> powr;

        cout << "The Answer is:  " << pow(numbr, powr);
}   // End of Main Function
```

Another built in function is the function that calculates the square root of a number, this function requires a single argument, which is the number that we will use for calculation and as with all value returning functions it requires a variable name in which to store the result returned from the function.

```
// square.cpp
#include<iostream>
#include<cmath>
using namespace std;
        void main()  {
                float numbr = (float) 36.0;  // the number
                float answr = (float) 0.0; // the answer

                answr = sqrt(numbr);

                cout << "The Answer is:  " << answr;
        }   // End of Main Function
```

We assign two variables of type float because we can expect a number with a fraction as an answer. The first, named numbr is where we will store the value that will be used to calculate the square root and the second, named answr is where the function will store the result when it returns.

The next instruction is where the calculation occurs. We will receive the result of the calculation in the variable named answr. To the right of the assignment operator we find the built-in function with one argument (or parameter). The argument which is the variable numbr is between the parenthesis and the contents will be used to calculate the square root.

The last statement in the program is where we output the answer. The string literal "The Answer is: " will be displayed on the screen followed by the contents of the variable named answr.

Lesson 17.4 SAMPLE PROGRAM

A sample C++ program is shown below. This program illustrates two of the built in functions, pow() and sqr().

```
// systemfunct.cpp
// Jim Kelley
// 6 November 2009
#include <iostream>
#include <cmath>

using namespace std;
int main()
{
    // declare variables
     double cube;
```

```
        double square;
        int i;
        for (i=1; i<10; i++)
        {
                cube = pow(static_cast<double>(i), 3);
                cout << cube << " ";
        }
        cout << endl;
        for (i=10; i<20; i++)
        {
                square = sqrt(static_cast<double>(i));
                cout << square << " ";
        }
        cout << endl;
}   // End of Main function
```

First, note the #include <cmath> directive. This is the library that contains the functions that we will use in our program, it will not work without this directive. Next, note the first for loop will loop ten times. Each loop will calculate the cube of the index number of the current iteration of the loop and display it on the common output. The second loop will square the index number of the loop which will begin with the number 10 and loop until the index is equal to the number 20, each time displaying the calculation to the common output device.

Lesson 17.5 Summary

C++ programs are built with functions. There is always at least one function, the main function. Every C++ compiler comes with a set of libraries of pre-written functions that are standard to all variations of C++. A function consists of a datatype, a function name, and a list of arguments or parameters(if required). Functions allow programmers to build solutions to problems or units of code that, once built, can be used repeatedly within the program or if put in a library, used by other programs. Learning to use functions is key to developing programs in many different modern programming languages.

End of Lesson Quiz

A _____ can be defined as a program or part of a program.

All C++ programs consist of at lease one function, that being the _____ function.

The function name is always followed by a set of _____.

Lesson 18
User Defined Functions - Value Returning Functions

Objectives:

- Explain use of User Defined Functions.
- Describe a Value Returning Function.
- Use value returning functions.
- Use function prototypes.
- Explain actual and formal parameters.

Lesson 18.1 USER DEFINED FUNCTIONS

While most C++ compilers have a rich library of built in functions, it is impossible to have all possible code requirements covered. Also, there are some real advantages to the ability to create your own functions.

One of the biggest advantages is to allow a large program to be divided up between several programmers. Another big benefit to functions is that it allows you to create the code to do a common task that will be used several times in the same program or in several programs. Once you test the code you can store that code and then use it in many other programs requiring the same code. Just like the originators of C++ wrote those built in functions, we can add to that library by adding our own functions.

As we begin our discussion of user defined functions we should remember that it is real tempting to continue to write programs like we have done since the beginning of the course all in the main function. With functions we need to change our thinking.

When we begin our analysis of the program we should pick out the functions FIRST. Each function we write should be set up in its own IPO chart, just as if it was its own unique program. If you are writing the whole program and function by yourself you should even consider writing the functions first.

In a later lesson we will talk more about how we can develop large programs using several programmers by assigning different functions to each programmer and how they will all fit together at the end.

Lesson 18.2 VALUE RETURNING FUNCTIONS

The value returning function returns a value to the calling program statement. This means having a variable, an output statement or an expression available to receive the value returned by the function. Let's look at a program segment that calls a value returning function called multno that multiplies a given number by 100:

```
int hinbr = 0;
numbr = 18;
hinbr = multno(numbr);
cout << "The new number is: " << hinbr;
```

Note the third line, this is the line that calls the function. It begins with a variable name to receive the returned value. This is followed by the assignment operator (=). Next is the name of the function (multno) which has the argument which is in this example, the contents of the variable named numbr, within the parenthesis. When the multno function is finished, it stores the value calculated (100 * 18) in the variable named hinbr and returns control to the next statement which prints the calculated value to the screen.

The function itself may look like this:

```
int multno(int nbrx) {
    int answr = 0;
    answr = nbrx * 100;
    return answr;
} // End of function multno()
```

The first line declares the type of data to be returned (int), the name of the function (multno) and the argument passed (int nbrx) as a datatype and a variable name. Note the variable name is not the same as used in the calling statement. It is not necessary to provide the same name as the function is only generating a copy for use within the function. It sets up a local variable in the function named nbrx of type int, initialized to the value passes which in this case is 18. The last part of the line contains the opening bracket for the functions statement block.

The second line declares a variable named answr and initializes it to zero. This is the variable in which we will calculate the value to be returned.

The third line does the calculation. The value passed from the calling program was copied into a variable named nbrx of datatype integer and this value is multiplied by the numeric literal 100, the resulting value is assigned to the variable name answr.

The fourth line uses the return keyword and this is the line that returns the value stored in answr to the calling function.

The fifth line contains the closing bracket for the statement block.

Lesson 18.3 FUNCTION PROTOTYPES

Functions may be placed before or after the main function, or even both before and after. It is a good convention to decide on either before or after the main function as it is often important in debugging to be able to quickly locate the main function.

As a matter of convention, well constructed programs add user functions after the main function. However, this presents a problem. When compiling the main function and encountering a user function, the compiler has no idea what the user function does or its parameters or any other necessary information. It then generates a not found error message. So, to prevent this problem, we put a copy of the function header immediately after the namespace command in the heading. Just copy the function header and add a semicolon at the end and you have the function prototype.

The function prototype for the multno() function from Lesson 18.2 would look like this:

```
int multno(int nbrx);
```

The prototype includes the datatype, the name of the function, the formal parameters enclosed in parentheses and ended with a semicolon.

Lesson 18.4 ACTUAL AND FORMAL PARAMETERS

We differentiate the parameters in the function call from the parameters in the function header and prototype with some more terminology. The parameters (or arguments if you choose that terminology) in the function call are termed ACTUAL PARAMETERS. Actual parameters refer to variables in the calling program and DO NOT require a data type. The parameters in the function header and the function prototype are called the FORMAL PARAMETERS. Formal Parameters require a data type in front of each variable name.

The ACTUAL PARAMETERS in the function call refer to the actual names of variables in the calling function. They are not preceded by a data type. This is the data or variable names being passed to the function call.

The FORMAL PARAMETERS are found in the prototype and the function header. They are preceded by a data type. They need not be the same names as found in the function call but each parameter must be in the same order as the call and must be of the same data type. These act as a variable definition for the function.

Lesson 18.5 SAMPLE PROGRAM

A sample C++ program is shown below. We are back to the payroll example. Now we will modify the various parts of the program and turn some of them into functions. This way we could use those functions as parts of other programs.

We are adding a function that receives the grosspay and the married character flag. If the married flag indicates married status the grosspay variable is multiplied by a factor of .16, if the flag indicates single the grosspay variable is multiplied by a factor of .08. The result of the multiplication is then subtracted from the grosspay and returned to the calling function.

```cpp
// pay1.cpp
// Date:
// Author:
#include <iostream>
#include <iomanip>
#include <string>
#include <fstream>

using namespace std;
// function prototypes
double marded(double grossPay, char married);

int main()
{
    // declare variables
    double hoursWorked = 0.0;
    double rateOfPay = 0.00;
    double grossPay = 0.0;
    string name;
    double fedTax = 0.0;
    double netPay = 0.0;
    char married = 'Y';
    int dep = 0;
    double deduct = 0.0;
    int health = 0;
    double price = 0.0;
    double depded = 0.0;
    int i;

    // declare input and output file streams
    ifstream inFile;
```

```
ofstream outFile;

// open the files for input and output
inFile.open("payin.txt");
outFile.open("payroll.dat");

// set format manipulators
cout << fixed << showpoint;
cout << setprecision(2);

// get input data from payin.txt
// priming read

inFile >> hoursWorked;

inFile >> rateOfPay;

inFile >> dep;

inFile >> married;

inFile >> health;

getline(inFile, name);

// Start Processing Loop

while (infile)
{
// processing statements
grossPay = hoursWorked * rateOfPay;

// call function to calculate deductions
grossPay = marded(grossPay, married);   // function call

// Deductions for dependents
depded = 0.0;
for (i = 1; i <= dep; i++)
 {
      depded = depded + 12.00;
 }


// determine the cost of the health package selected.
// this is a pretax deduction
switch(health)
    {
    case 0:
       grossPay = grossPay - 0;
       price = 0.0;
       break;
    case 1:
       grossPay = grossPay - 18.00;
       price = 18.00;
       break;
    case 2:
       grossPay = grossPay - 22.00;
       price = 22.00;
       break;
```

```cpp
         case 3:
            grossPay = grossPay - 28.00;
            price = 28.00;
            break;
         case 4:
            grossPay = grossPay - 33.00;
            price = 33.00;
            break;
         default:
            grossPay = grossPay - 0;
            price = 0.0;
       }   // end of switch statement



   // decide how much federal tax the employee should pay
   // next 4 lines: demonstrate the single sided if statement
   if (grossPay <= 400.00)
       fedTax = grossPay * .12;
   if (grossPay > 400.00)
       fedTax = grossPay * .18;



   // calculate the net pay
   netPay = grossPay - fedTax - deduct;

   // display the result
   outFile << "Weekly Pay for: " << setw(6) << name << endl;
   outFile << "Gross Pay:       " << setw(6) << grossPay << endl;
   outFile << "Hours Worked:    " << setw(6) << hoursWorked << endl;
   outFile << "Rate of Pay:     " << setw(6) << rateOfPay << endl;
   outFile << "Married:         " << setw(6) << married << endl;
   outFile << "Dependents:      " << setw(6) << dep << endl;
   outFile << "Deductions:      " << setw(6) << deduct + depded << endl;
   outFile << "Health:          " << setw(6) << price << endl;
   outFile << "Federal Tax:     " << setw(6) << fedTax << endl;
   outFile << "Net Pay:         " << setw(6) << netPay << endl;

   // Read Next Record from the input file
   // get input data from payin.txt

   inFile >> hoursWorked;

   inFile >> rateOfPay;

   inFile >> dep;

   inFile >> married;

   inFile >> health;

   getline(inFile, name);

   } // End of While loop

   inFile.close();
   outFile.close();
   return 0;
```

```
}       // end of main function

  double marded(double grossPay, char married)
    {
     double fact = 0.0;
     double ded = 0.0;
     // use if to determine married / single deductions
     if (married = 'Y')
        {
         fact = .16;
         ded = grossPay * fact;
        }
     else
        {
         fact = .08;
         ded = grossPay * fact;
        }
     return grossPay - ded;
    }  // end of function marded
```

Lesson 18.6 Summary

The concept of user defined functions can enhance program development. In this section we examine value returning functions and void functions. This lesson concentrates on value returning functions.

As the name implies, value returning functions return a value to the calling functions. This makes it necessary that the calling function be prepared to receive a value that may be stored in a variable, written to an output device or used in an equation or expression.

The three elements we need are (1) the prototype that identifies the function and its arguments to the main or calling function. (2) The function call that provides a plan to receive the value returned, the function name and the list of actual arguments. (3) The function that includes a datatype of the value to be returned, the name of the function and the list of formal arguments. This is followed by the function statements enclosed in curly braces.

End of Lesson Quiz

A _____ _____ function returns a value to the calling program statement.

The first part of the function header is a _____ _____.

The parameters in the function call are referred to as the _____ parameters.

The parameters in the function header are referred to as the _____ parameters.

Lesson 19
User Defined Functions - Void Functions

Objectives:

- Explain use of Void Functions.
- Describe a void Function.
- Use void functions.

Lesson 19.1 VOID FUNCTIONS

By definition a void function is a function that does not return a value. The void function may do some processing or some task and then return to the next statement in the calling program after the statement that called the function. Void functions are usually used for those tasks that do not return a value or values to the calling function. For example, lets look at a segment of code that calls a void function that prints page headings called pagehead():

```
pageno  = pageno + 1;    // add 1 to page  counter
pagehead(pageno);        // pass pageno to the pagehead function
lineno  = 4;             // next  instruction after function returns
```

The first line increments a variable named pageno by one. The second line is the line that calls the void function. It consists of the name of the function followed by a set of parenthesis containing a variable name. This is called a function argument or parameter. It is a value that the function requires to do its job. In this instance it will contain the page number to be printed in the heading. A copy of this variable will be passed to the function and the original value of the variable will never be changed by the function.

The function itself may look something like this:

```
void pagehead(int pageno)
 {
     cout << "==========Acme Inc.===========" << endl;
     cout << "Page Number: " <<  pageno << endl;
 }      // End of Function pagehead()
```

The first line declares the type of function (void), the name of the function (pagehead) and the argument passed by name and data type (int pageno). This argument creates a copy of the data being passed in a variable named pageno with a data type of integer. Lastly the beginning bracket showing the start of the statement block associated with the function.

The second and third lines put out the two heading lines.

The fourth line is the closing bracket showing the end of the statement block.

Lesson 19.2 USING VOID FUNCTIONS

Note the function call for a void function is just the function name followed by any necessary arguments in parenthesis. Generally, we do not use void functions to return data or results of calculations to the calling function. Void functions do a task and usually do not involve calculations. A good example of using void functions is placement of headings or footers on reports. A heading and footer can be designed to work for many different reports, and when properly coded, can be ported to every program that requires a heading or footer without extensive programming and testing.

Another good use for a void function is to output a menu of choices for the user, rather than code this in the main function itself. Here is an example of a program that calls a void function to give the user a menu of choices:

```cpp
// menu.cpp
// author: J.Kelley
// March 3, 2008
#include<iostream>
using namespace std;

// function prototype
void menuchoice();

int main()
{
// declare variables
int choice = 0;
// call function to display menu.
menuchoice();              // function call
// get user choice
cin >> choice;
// display choice
cout << "Your choice was: " << choice << endl;
return 0;
}       // End of Main Function

// now the function menuchoice
void menuchoice()
{
        cout << "1 = Choice number one " << endl;
        cout << "2 = Choice number two " << endl;
        cout << "3 = Exit the program  " << endl;
}       // end of menuchoice function
```

Also, worthy of noting is that in the function there is NO return statement. Void functions do not directly return a value. There is a prototype required that, just like the value returning function, looks exactly like the function header ended by a semicolon.

Lesson 19.3 PASSING PARAMETERS TO VOID FUNCTIONS

All functions, void or value returning may or may not require parameters (or arguments). Arguments or parameters, whichever you call them (both mean exactly the same thing) are simply a means for passing information from one function to another.

Formal arguments (or parameters) are the arguments shown in the prototype and the function heading. These arguments have data types attached. You may see prototypes with only the data types indicated and this is all that is actually required. The arguments in the function header must have both a data type and a variable name for each argument.

Actual arguments (or parameters) are the arguments shown in the function call. These each represent an actual variable in the calling function. These must be in the same order as indicated by the function header and must match the data types exactly.

When passing arguments to functions, you must remember that order is important. The arguments passed to the function must be in the order expected by the function.

```
EXAMPLE OF CORRECT ARGUMENT PASSING

        void rpthead(string name, int pgno, int pgct, string co);   // prototype

    IN MAIN FUNCTION:
            int pgno = 1;
            int pgct = 1;
            string name = "Pay Report";
            string co = "Acme, Inc.";

            rpthead(name, pgno, pgct, co);   // function call

    FUNCTION:
    void rpthead(string name, int pgno, int pgct, string co)
    {
            statement(s);
    }

EXAMPLE OF INCORRECT ARGUMENT PASSING

        void rpthead(string name, int pgno, int pgct, string co);   // prototype

    IN MAIN FUNCTION:
            int pgno = 1;
            int pgct = 1;
            string name = "Pay Report";
            string co = "Acme, Inc.";

            rpthead(pgno, pgct, name, co);   // function call

    FUNCTION:
    void rpthead(string name, int pgno, int pgct, string co)
    {
            statement(s);
    }
```

Note that in the incorrect example, the variable names in the function call do not match the order of variables in the function prototype and the function call. Having the order of the parameters match in the prototype, the call and the header is required for the function to work correctly.

Lesson19.4 SAMPLE PROGRAM

To our payroll program we add a void function that will place a report heading consisting of the report name and the page number in front of every three employee reports.

In our sample program we call a void function with two arguments, one for the name of the report and the other for the page number to be printed on the page. Both of these variables must be placed a the top of each of 3 different employee reports so the function must be reusable.

```
// pay1.cpp
// Date:
// Author:
#include <iostream>
#include <iomanip>
#include <string>
#include <fstream>
```

```cpp
using namespace std;

// function prototypes
double marded(double grossPay, char married, double deduct);
void newPage(ofstream& outFile, int pageno, string reportname);

int main()
{
    // declare variables
    double hoursWorked = 0.0;
    double rateOfPay = 0.00;
    double grossPay = 0.0;
    string name;
    double fedTax = 0.0;
    double netPay = 0.0;
    char married = 'Y';
    int dep = 0;
    double deduct = 0.0;
    int health = 0;
    double price = 0.0;
    double depded = 0.0;
    int i;
    string reportname = "Payroll Report - Bigg Enterprises, Inc.";
    int pageno = 0;
    int lineno = 0;

    // declare input and output file streams
    ifstream inFile;
    ofstream outFile;

    // open the files for input and output
    inFile.open("payin.txt");
    outFile.open("payroll.dat");

    // set format manipulators
    cout << fixed << showpoint;
    cout << setprecision(2);

    // get input data from payin.txt
    // priming read

    inFile >> hoursWorked;

    inFile >> rateOfPay;

    inFile >> dep;

    inFile >> married;

    inFile >> health;

    getline(inFile, name);

    // Start Processing Loop

    while (inFile)
    {
    // processing statements
    grossPay = hoursWorked * rateOfPay;
```

```
// call function to calculate deductions
grossPay = marded(grossPay, married, deduct);   // function call

// Deductions for dependents
depded = 0.0;
for (i = 1; i <= dep; i++)
 {
        depded = depded + 12.00;
 }


// determine the cost of the health package selected.
// this is a pretax deduction
switch(health)
    {
    case 0:
       grossPay = grossPay - 0;
       price = 0.0;
       break;
    case 1:
       grossPay = grossPay - 18.00;
       price = 18.00;
       break;
    case 2:
       grossPay = grossPay - 22.00;
       price = 22.00;
       break;
    case 3:
       grossPay = grossPay - 28.00;
       price = 28.00;
       break;
    case 4:
       grossPay = grossPay - 33.00;
       price = 33.00;
       break;
    default:
       grossPay = grossPay - 0;
       price = 0.0;
    }




// decide how much federal tax the employee should pay
// next 4 lines: demonstrate the single sided if statement
if (grossPay <= 400.00)
    fedTax = grossPay * .12;
if (grossPay > 400.00)
    fedTax = grossPay * .18;




// calculate the net pay
netPay = grossPay - fedTax - deduct;

// display the result
lineno++;
if (lineno > 3)     // start new page after 3 employees
{
```

```cpp
            lineno = 0;
            pageno++;
            newPage(outFile, pageno, reportname);
        }
        outFile << "Weekly Pay for: " << setw(6) << name << endl;
        outFile << "Gross Pay:      " << setw(6) << grossPay << endl;
        outFile << "Hours Worked:   " << setw(6) << hoursWorked << endl;
        outFile << "Rate of Pay:    " << setw(6) << rateOfPay << endl;
        outFile << "Married:        " << setw(6) << married << endl;
        outFile << "Dependents:     " << setw(6) << dep << endl;
        outFile << "Deductions:     " << setw(6) << deduct + depded << endl;
        outFile << "Health:         " << setw(6) << price << endl;
        outFile << "Federal Tax:    " << setw(6) << fedTax << endl;
        outFile << "Net Pay:        " << setw(6) << netPay << endl;

        // Read Next Record from the input file
        // get input data from payin.txt
        inFile >> hoursWorked;

        inFile >> rateOfPay;

        inFile >> dep;

        inFile >> married;

        inFile >> health;

        getline(inFile, name);

        } // End of While loop
        inFile.close();
        outFile.close();
        return 0;
}        // end of main function

    double marded(double grossPay, char married, double deduct)
        {
        // use if to determine married / single deductions
        double fact = 0.0;
        double ded = 0.0;
        if (married = 'Y')
            {
            fact = .16;
            ded = grossPay * fact;
            }
        else
            {
            deduct = .08;
            ded = grossPay * fact;
            }
        return grossPay - ded;
        }        // end of marded function

void newPage(ofstream& outFile, int pageno, string reportname)
{
    outFile << endl;
    outFile << endl;
    outFile << reportname << setw(6) << pageno << endl;
    outFile << endl;
```

```
}       // end of newPage function
```

Lesson19.5 Summary

Void functions are usually used to perform some task like print a heading, display a menu, put a record to an output file, etc.. As in the value returning functions they required a prototype, a function call as well as the function itself. Note, the void function does not return a value so the return statement is not required. Also, the function call does not need to account for a returned value.

End of Lesson Quiz

A _____ function does not return a value.

When passing arguments (parameters) to functions, you must remember that _____ is important.

Unlike the value returning function, the void function does not require a _____ statement.

Lesson 20
User Defined Functions - Pass by Value vs. Pass by Reference

Objectives:

- Explain the use of Pass by Value.
- Explain the use of Pass by Reference.
- Create a function that uses pass by value.
- Create a function that uses pass by reference.
- Create a function that uses both pass by reference and value.
- Use pass by reference in a void function.

Lesson 20.1 PASS BY VALUE

There are two ways to pass arguments from one function to another, pass by value and pass by reference. First we will discuss the pass by value method of passing data.

Pass by value does exactly what it implies, passes a value to a function. It passes a copy of the actual value indicated by the argument (or parameter) to the function. What this means is that the function cannot change the original value of argument passed to the function. The function call sends a list of values to the function. In the function header we have declared a space for each value passed along with the appropriate data type. This allows the function to "declare" these variables for use in the function. The names of variables in the function call (actual arguments) need not match the names of the variables declared in the function header (formal arguments). However, order of arguments is important. Let's look at an example:

```cpp
// passbyvalue.cpp
// Date:
// Author:
#include<iostream>
using namespace std;

// function prototype
double interest(double amount, double rate, double term);

int main()
{
    // declare variables
    double principal = 1000;
    double intrate = 0.0525;
    double term = 1.0;
    double intgr = 0.0;
    // call function interest
    intgr = interest(principal, intrate, term);  // function call
    // print the answer
    cout << "The calculated interest is: " << intgr << endl;
    return 0;
}    // end of main function

double interest(double amount, double rate, double term)
{
    // note we can put the entire formula
    // in the return statement
    return amount * rate * term;
}    // end of interest function
```

The interest function requires three parameters. The first a type double indicating the amount on which we will calculate the interest. The second argument is the rate of interest to be used in the calculation expressed as a decimal. The third and last argument is the term of the loan, the number of years required to pay back the loan. The arguments in the call must be in the same order as expected by the function and must be of the same data type.

Lesson 20.2 PASS BY REFERENCE

The second way to pass arguments from one function to another is to pass by reference. Pass by reference differs from pass by value in that with pass by reference you are passing a pointer to the variable in the calling function to the function thus allowing the called functions to use the original data in the calling function. In our example below we took the same scenario as we used in pass by value and converted it to pass by reference. First we changed the function type from double to void. Remember, void functions cannot return a value so if it is necessary for a void function to return a value we can accomplish this by using pass by reference. Pass by reference is indicated in both the function prototype and the function header by including a "&" character immediately following the data type. It is not necessary to indicate pass by reference in the function call. So, to accomplish this in our example, we add one parameter to our function to allow us to pass by reference the variable int to the function. First let's examine the code and then pick it apart.

```cpp
// passbyref.cpp
// Date:
// Author:
#include<iostream>
using namespace std;

// function prototype
void interest(double& intgr, double amount, double rate, double term);

int main()
{
    // declare variables
    double principal = 1000;
    double intrate = 0.0525;
    double term = 1.0;
    double intgr = 0.0;
    // call function interest
    interest(intgr, principal, intrate, term);  // function call
    // print the answer
    cout << "The calculated interest is: " << intgr << endl;
    return 0;
}    // end of main function

void interest(double& intgr, double amount, double rate, double term)
{
    // intgr in the main function will contain the result
    intgr = amount * rate * term;
}    // end of interest function
```

First, how does pass by reference work? When we did pass by value, we passed a copy of the data to the function and the function could not affect the data in the variables in the calling program. Pass by reference does it a little differently. It does not pass a copy of the data to the function but, rather the address of (or pointer to) the variable in the calling function. This allows the function to work directly with the data in the calling program. In our example above, we added the variable *intgr* as pass by reference and this allowed us to do the calculation in the void function and place the answer back in the calling program in the variable named intgr. This is all possible because the pass by reference passed a pointer back to the variable address in the calling program and allowed the function to store the answer at that location.

Lesson 20.3 PASS BY REFERENCE IN VALUE RETURNING FUNCTIONS

Pass by reference works in value returning functions exactly like it did in the above void function example. The benefit here is that it allows a value returning function to return more than one value. This allows us to return one value with the return statement and others via the pass by reference in the parameters. The only danger being that when a function alters the contents of variables in a calling function is that the integrity of the data in the calling function is not maintained. A big disadvantage of pass by reference is that it makes it more difficult to write functions that can be shared by many different programs. Our sample program will show examples of both pass by value and pass by reference for both value returning functions as well as void functions.

Lesson 20.4 SAMPLE PROGRAM

This week we leave our continuing payroll example to illustrate different principles. A sample C++ program is shown below that illustrates pass by value, pass by reference in both value returning functions and void functions. The void function calculates the perimeter of a rectangle given the length and the width and place it in a variable in the calling function named perimeter, passed by reference. The value returning function calculates he area and passes the answer back to the calling function in a return statement.

```cpp
// valandref.cpp
// Date:
// Author:
#include<iostream>
using namespace std;

// function prototypes
void perim(int& perimeter, int length, int width);
int sqarea(int length, int width, double& sqyard);

int main()
{
    // declare variables
    int length = 100;
    int width = 80;
    double sqyard = 0;
    int perimeter = 0;
    int area = 0;

    // call void function perim
    perim(perimeter, length, width);  // function call

    // call value returning function area
    area = sqarea(length, width, sqyard);

    // print the answers
    cout << "The calculated perimeter is:    " << perimeter << endl;
    cout << "The calculated area is:         " << area << endl;
    cout << "The calculated square yards is: " << sqyard << endl;
    return 0;
}       // end of main function
```

```
void perim(int& perimeter, int length, int width)
{
        // int in the main function will contain the result
        perimeter = (length + width) * 2;
}       // end of perim function

int sqarea(int length, int width, double& sqyard)
{
        int area;
        // calculate the area
        area = length * width;
        // calculate the square yards and return by reference
        sqyard = static_cast<double>(length * width) / 3.0;
        // area in the main function will contain the result
        return area;
}       // end of sqarea function
```

Lesson 20.5 Summary

There are two ways to pass arguments from one function to another, pass by value and pass by reference. Pass by value passes a copy of the contents of a variable to the function, keeping the integrity of the value in the variable of the calling function.

Pass by reference allows the calling function to pass a pointer to a variable so the function can work with the original value. This allows the called function to change the contents of one or more variables in the calling function.

The disadvantages of pass by reference are that the original values in the calling program are changed and using pass by reference makes the functions much less useful if it is to be used in other programs. So, pass by reference should only be used for instances where it is absolutely necessary.

End of Lesson Quiz

There are two ways to pass arguments (parameters) to a function, pass by _____ and pass by _____.

Pass by _____ passes a copy of the actual values.

Pass by _____ passes a pointer to the value in the calling function.

Pass by reference is indicated in both the function prototype and the function header by including a _____ character immediately following the _____ _____.

Lesson 21
User Defined Functions
Void vs. Value Returning Functions and Nested Functions

Objectives:
- Differentiate void and value returning functions.
- Explain when to use each type of function.
- Code nested functions.

Lesson 21.1 VOID vs VALUE RETUNING FUNCTIONS

When do I use a void function and when do I use a value returning function? Why are there two types of functions? These are questions asked by those learning C++. Usually those who have little prior programming experience. However, these are valid questions. This lesson will attempt to answer these questons.

First, when to use a void function. By definition a void function does not return a value. It is designed to perform a task that is used repeatedly in a program or group of programs. It may be used to print a line in a report that is repeated often, a heading, a footer, a separator line of asterisks or dashes, or a menu of choices. These are just a few of the many uses of the void function. If is not intended to do calculation or other tasks that need to return results to the calling function. Let's look at a program that asks the user for a number between 5 and 9 and then uses a function to print out that number of asterisks.

```cpp
// asterisks.cpp
// Date:
// Author:
// Example of a void function

#include<iostream>
using namespace std;

// function prototypes
void line(int nbr);

int main()
{
    // declare variables
    int number1 = 0;

    //ask user for a number 5 to 9
    cout << "Enter a number between 5 and 9 ";
    cin >> number1;
    if (number1 < 5 || number1 > 9)
    {
        cout << "BAD INPUT" << endl;
        return 1;
    }

    // call the function
    line(number1);

    // end the program
    cout << "Program Completed" << endl;
    return 0;
```

```
}       // end of main function

void line(int nbr)
{
      int i;
      for (i = 1; i <= nbr; i++)
      {
            cout << "*";
      }
}       // end of line function
```

The main function asks the user for a number between 5 and 9. Yes, after the cin statement we should verify that the user entered a number in the correct range. The main function then calls the **line** function and passes the number entered by value. The line function then uses the information for the limit to the number of asterisks to be printed by the for loop.

A value returning function is used when the function is designed to do a calculation or some other task that returns a value to the calling function. Calculating simple interest is an often used example for illustrating a value returning function. The calling program passes the arguments for amount of the loan, the interest percentage and the term of the loan. The interest function returns the calculated interest.

```
// interest.cpp
// Date:
// Author:
// Example of a value returning function

#include<iostream>
using namespace std;

// function prototypes
double interest(double amount, double rate, double term);

int main()
{
      // declare variables
      double loan = 0.0;
      double intrate = 0.0;
      double term = 0.0;
      double intamt = 0.0;

      //ask user for data
      cout << "Enter loan amount: ";
      cin >> loan;
      cout << "Enter interest rate: ";
      cin >> intrate;
      cout << "Enter years of loan: ";
      cin >> term;

      // call the function
      intamt = interest(loan, intrate, term);

      // end the program
      cout << "The interest is: " << intamt << endl;
      cout << "Program Completed" << endl;
      return 0;
}       // end of main function
```

```
double interest(double amount, double rate, double term)
{
        return (amount * rate * term);
}       // end of line function
```

Next, why are there two types of functions? This answer is a little more difficult. We have learned many different things about functions that would allow us to write either type of function to accomplish the same tasks. Perhaps the biggest difference is that when you see a void function and it is used properly you expect that it will not be doing a calculation or returning a value. A quick glance at the prototype will tell you if it uses any pass by reference arguments which will be the only way it will affect anything in the calling program. Pass by Value functions will always return a value of the same data type as in the function header. You expect a value returning function to be used in some type of calculation or for a task that will return a value to the calling function.

Lesson 21.2 NESTED FUNCTIONS

To this point we have only looked at functions called by the main function and technically this is one function nested within a second function(the main function). Let's look at the main function that calls a function which then calls a third function. The main function will call a value returning function which will in turn call another value returning function. Note that a value returning function may call a void function or vice versa.

```
// nested.cpp
// author: J Kelley
// Date: March 4, 2008
//
#include<iostream>
using namespace std;

// function prototypes
double calcbill(double amount, double qty, double rate);
double taxcalc(double amt, double taxrate);

int main()
{
        // declare variables
        double amount = 0.0;
        double rate = 0.0;
        double qty = 0.0;
        double total = 0.0;

        // ask user for inputs
        cout << "Enter the cost per piece ordered: ";
        cin >> amount;
        cout << "Enter the quantity ordered:        ";
        cin >> qty;
        cout << "Enter the local tax rate:          ";
        cin >> rate;

        // calculate the total
        total = calcbill(amount, qty, rate);   // function call

        // display the answer
        cout >> "The total bill is: " << total << endl;
        return 0;
}       // end of main function
```

```
double calcbill(double amount, double qty, double rate)
{
        double totalamt = 0.0;
        totalamt = (amount * qty);
        totalamt += taxcalc(totalamt, rate);   // function call
        return totalamt;
}        // end of calcbill function

double taxcalc(double amt, double taxrate)
{
        double tottax = 0.0;
        tottax = amt + (amt * taxrate);
        return tottax;
}        // end of taxcalc function
```

The main function calls the calcbill function passing three arguments. After the calcbill function calculates the totalamt it calls the taxcalc function to calculate the tax. The taxcalc function returns the tax amount to calc blll and the totalamt is returned to the main function.

Lesson 21.3 SAMPLE PROGRAM

A sample C++ program is shown below. The intent of this program is to demonstrate the use of nested void and value returning functions and in no way represents an actual tax situation. Note how the main function calls one of two value returning functions and then displays the results by calling a void function which, in turn, calls another void function.

```
// taxes.cpp
// Date:
// Author:
//
#include<iostream>
#include<string>
using namespace std;

// function prototypes
double unmarr(double gross, int dep, double insure, int married);
double marr(double gross, int dep, double insure, int married);
void printtax(double netpay, double grossPay, double hours, double rate);
double calcdepded(double dep, int married);
void printhead(string name, string rptdate);

int main()
{
        // declare variables
        double hours = 0.0;
        double rate = 0.0;
        double grossPay = 0.0;
        int depn = 0;
        double insurance = 0.0;
        double netpay = 0.0;
        int married = 0;

        // have user enter information
        cout << "Hours:                     ";
        cin >> hours;
        cout << "Pay Rate:                  ";
        cin >> rate;
```

```cpp
        cout << "Dependents:                       ";
        cin >> depn;
        cout << "Married 1 = yes/ 2 = no:     ";
        cin >> married;

        // calculate gross pay
        grossPay = hours * rate;

        // calculate taxes
        if (married == 1)
                netpay = marr(grossPay, depn, insurance, married);  // call
        else
                netpay = unmarr(grossPay, depn, insurance, married); // call

        // display results
        printtax(netpay, grossPay, hours, rate);  // function call
        return 0;
}       // end of main function

double unmarr(double gross, int dep, double insure, int married)
{
        // declare variables
        double tottax = 0.0;
        double depded = 0.0;
        // calculate deductions
        depded = calcdepded(dep, 2); // a nested function
        // calculate total tax and return
        return (gross - depded - insure);
}       // end of unmarr function

double marr(double gross, int dep, double insure, int married)
{
        // declare variables
        double tottax = 0.0;
        double depded = 0.0;
        // calculate deductions
        depded = calcdepded(dep, 1); // a nested function
        // calculate total tax and return
        return (gross - depded - insure);
}       // end of marr function

void printtax(double netpay, double grossPay, double hours, double rate)
{
        printhead("Bigg-Time, LTD.", "March 5, 2013");
        cout << netpay << "  " << grossPay << "  " << hours << "  " << rate << endl;
}       // end of printtax function

void printhead(string name, string rptdate)
{
        cout << name << "  " << rptdate << endl;
}       // end of printhead function

double calcdepded(double dep, int married)
{
        double depded = 0.0;
        if (dep > 3)
                depded = dep * 10;
        else
                depded = dep * 20;
```

```
        return depded / married;
}       // end of calcdepded function
```

Lesson 21.4 Summary

Proper use of a void function is a task that does not return a value to a calling function. If the function needs to return one or more values, use a value returning function with pass by reference to return the extra values.

Any function may call another function. A value returning function may call a void function or vice versa. The deeper the nesting of functions the more difficult it will be to debug the program and reusability of the function may be a problem.

End of Lesson Quiz

There are two types of functions, pass by _____ and pass by _____.

A _____ function does not return a value.

A function within another function may be referred to as a _____ function.

Lesson 22
User Defined Functions
Programming with Functions a Review.

Objectives:
- Explain use of Void Functions.
- Explain use of Value Returning Functions.
- Describe when to use each type of function.
- Describe pass by value and pass by reference.
- List various programming techniques for functions.

Lesson 22.1 VOID AND VALUE RETURNING FUNCTIONS

In review, we now know that a void function does not return a value to the calling program and is generally used to do some type of task like print out information. In contrast, the value returning functions are designed to return a value to the calling program and are generally used to do calculations and tasks that normally would result in information to be passed back to the calling program.

There are three (3) areas of functions; function prototypes; function calls; and function headers. Function headers and function prototypes contain exactly the same data. Each start with a data type (or void), then a function name followed by the Formal Parameters enclosed in parenthesis. In the case of the prototype the line is ended with a semicolon. In the case of a function header it does NOT end with a semicolon but is followed by an open curly brace ({), followed by the function statements and ended with a closing curly brace (}). All types of functions, except the void type, must have a return statement that is the last statement executed in the function. There may be multiple return statements in a function. The function statement returns a single value of the data type of the function.

Function calls are slightly different. The function call for a void function is simply the name of the function followed by the Actual parameters that will be passed to the function. The line containing the function call for a value returning function must have a place to store the value returned or display the function results. Then the function call is followed by the Actual Parameters that will be passed to the function.

```cpp
#include<iostream>
#include<string>
using namespace std;

// function prototypes
double taxcalc(double amount, double rate);
void printline(string name, string date, double tax);

int main()
{
    // declare variables
    double amount = 100.00;
    double rate = 0.05;
    double tax = 0.0;
    string name = "Large Purchase ";
    string date = "March 5, 2013";

    // call taxcalc value returning function
    tax = taxcalc(amount, rate);
```

```
            // call printline void function
            printline(name, date, tax);
            return 0;
    }       // end of main function


    double taxcalc(double amount, double rate)
    {
            return amount * rate;
    }       // end of taxcalc function
    void printline(string name, string date, double tax)
    {
            cout << name << "   " << date << "   ";
            cout "Tax is: " << tax << endl;
    }       // end of printline function
```

Lesson 22.2 PASS BY VALUE and PASS BY REFERENCE

Passing information to functions can be accomplished in two different ways, pass by value or pass by reference. Let's look at these two methods, when to use each and why each is important to C++ programming.

First, pass by value. Use pass by value when you want to send a copy of the information to the function that does not allow the function to affect the original value. The formal parameters in the function header set up variables of the appropriate data type to be used as long as processing remains in the function. Once the flow of the program leaves the function these variables cease to exist and their content is lost.

Pass by Reference. Use pass by reference when you want the function to have access to the contents of a variable in the calling function and allow the called function to change the value contained in that variable. You would use this when you want to return a value from a void function or when you need to return more than one value from a value returning function.

```
    #include<iostream>
    #include<string>
    #include<iomanip>

    using namespace std;

    // function prototypes
    double pmtcalc(double& amount, double loan, double rate, int term);
    void printmenu(int& choice);

    int main()
    {
            // declare variables
            double amount = 0.0;
            double loan = 20000.00;
            double rate = 0.10;
            double payment = 0.0;
            int term60 = 60;
            int term72 = 72;
            int choice = 0;
```

```
        // call menu function
        printmenu(choice);

        if (choice == 1)
                payment = pmtcalc(amount, loan, rate, term60);
        else
                payment = pmtcalc(amount, loan, rate, term72);

        // print results
        cout << fixed << showpoint;
        cout << setprecision(2);
        cout << "Loan Amount            " << loan << endl;
        cout << "Loan Rate              " << rate << endl;
        cout << "Payment                " << payment << endl;
        cout << "Total Amount of Payments " << amount << endl;
        return 0;
}       // end of main function

double pmtcalc(double& amount, double loan, double rate, int term)
{
        amount = loan + (loan * rate * (term / 12));
        return amount / term;
}       // end of pmtcalc function

void printmenu(int& choice)
{
        cout << "      Main Menu        " << endl;
        cout << " 1  Loan for 60 months" << endl;
        cout << " 2  Loan for 72 months" << endl;
        cout << endl;
        cin >> choice;
}       // end of printmenu function
```

The function named pmtcalc returns a value to the payment variable and because the amount variable is passed by reference it places the total payments into that variable in the main function.

The void function printmenu prints a menu with two choices and then waits for a user choice. Since there is no return statement we had to pass the variable choice as pass by reference. When the function completes, it stores the user response back in the variable choice in the calling program.

Lesson 22.3 PROGRAMMING WITH FUNCTIONS

There are several approaches to programming with functions. We always begin by carefully defining each function before any programming begins. We need to be clear on what each function will require in parameters and what the function will return to the calling program. This is especially important if we intend to reuse these functions in other programs. Then, the choice is to develop each function including the main function by a team of programmers, or all code done by the same programmer, Should you code the functions first or code the main function first?

Single programmer approach:
Our experience in this course has been the single programmer approach. One programmer codes

the main function and all the sub functions. This is great for the smaller tasks but for the large industrial strength applications this is not how it will operate. However, the team tools like function stubs will work well for the individual programmer as well as the team of programmers.

You should not overlook the possibility of developing functions that may be re-used in other programs. Program and test once, then use in subsequent programs. This is probably one of the biggest benefits of writing functions.

The team approach:
On very large programs it is not uncommon to have a program divided into sections that will be completed by different programmers. This calls for a very high level of planning. This is why we teach you pseudocode, flowcharts, IPO charts and other planning methods before you begin programming. In the "real world" these planning tools are a necessity. Proper planning is the only way all the pieces of a program will fit together and work flawlessly when completed in the team approach. Hopefully, by now you have figured out that functions play an important role in dividing up a program between programmers.

Again, in many situations, there will be a library of functions that have been written by the company that must be used for parts of every program produced. They may have standard report headers and footers that will be generated by functions. There may be complex calculations that have been solved by prior programmers in functions. All of this reuse of code adds up to savings on programming and testing time. To any company, time is money.

Function Stubs:
Function stubs is a technique that allows you to write and test parts of the program without having to have all the components ready before testing. Function stubs rely on having everything properly defined before beginning programming. Any changes made after the planning phase may have disasterous effects on some or all of the programmers involved in the project. Let's take a look at some of the different example code using function stubs.

```cpp
#include<iostream>
#include<string>
using namespace std;

// function prototypes
double interest(double principal, double rate, int term);

int main()
{
        // declare variables
        double principal = 0.0;
        double rate = 0.0;
        int term = 0;
        double simpleint = 0.0;

        // get data from the user
        cout << "Enter principal:            ";
        cin >> principal;
        cout << "Enter interest rate:        ";
        cin >> rate;
        cout << "Enter term in years:        ";
        cin >> term;

        // call the function
        simpleint = interest(principal, rate, term);
```

```
        // display the result
        cout << "The simple interest on this loan is: " << simpleint << endl;
        return 0;
} // end of main function

        // function stub for interest that returns 123.45
        double interest(double principal, double rate, int term)
        {
                return 123.45
        } // end of interest function
```

When the program executes properly, returning the expected results, we continue to add the required functions, one by one. Another scenario is that the functions may be programmed simultaneously by other programmers.

Now program the full function.

```
        // interest function
        double interest(double principal, double rate, int term)
        {
                return principal * rate * term;
        } // end of interest function
```

Yes, this function was hardly worth a second programmer but it allows the programmer to test the main function with a known value to insure accuracy. Once the program tests properly, then introduce the full function to do the calculation and return the calculated value. Also, most functions written in the "real world" are not this simple. Often they are a program by themselves and may require as much or more time to complete than the main function.

Lesson 22.4 SAMPLE PROGRAM

A sample C++ program is shown below. The intent of this program is to demonstrate using functions for more than one calculation. Each of the type double functions are used to calculate the cost and the price of the units in a case or in the warehouse. We can do this because cost and price are both type double that represent currency. The difference is on the calling function end where we store the returned values to different variables.

```
// inven.cpp
// Date:
// Author:
//
#include<iostream>
using namespace std;

// function prototypes
double invencostprice(int inven, double amount);
double kasecostprice(int kase, double amount);
void printreport(int inven, double invencost, double invenprice, int kase,
double casecost, double caseprice);

int main()
{
        // declare variables
        int inven = 0;
        int kase= 0;
        double cost = 0.0;
```

```cpp
    double price = 0.0;
    double invencost = 0.0;
    double invenprice = 0.0;
    double casecost = 0.0;
    double caseprice = 0.0;

    // have user enter information
    cout << "Enter the number of product in the warehouse    ";
    cin >> inven;
    cout << "Enter the number of product in a kase           ";
    cin >> kase;
    cout << "Enter cost to produce the item                  ";
    cin >> cost;
    cout << "Enter the wholesale price of the item           ";
    cin >> price;

    // calculate inventory cost and price
        invencost = invencostprice(inven, cost);
        invenprice = invencostprice(inven, price);

    // calculate casecost and price
        casecost = kasecostprice(kase, cost);
        caseprice = kasecostprice(kase, price);

    // display results
        printreport(inven, invencost, invenprice, kase, casecost, caseprice);
        return 0;
}       // end of main function


double invencostprice(int inven, double amount)
{
        double amt;
            amt = amount * inven;
        return amt;
}       // end of invencostprice function


double kasecostprice(int kase, double amount)
{
        double amt;
        amt = amount * case
        return amt;
}       // end of kasecostprice function


void printreport(int inven, double invencost, double invenprice,
int kase, double casecost, double caseprice)
{
        cout << "There are " << inven << " items in inventory " << endl;
        cout << "The cost of these items was " << invencost << endl;
        cout << "The retail of these items is " << invenprice << endl;
        cout << endl;
        cout << "There are " << kase << " items in a case" << endl;
        cout << "The cost of these items is " << casecost << endl;
        cout << "The retail of a case of these items is " << caseprice << endl;
        cout << endl;
}       // end of printreport function
```

Lesson 22.5 Summary

Void functions do not return values, they perform some type of task like printing a line. Value returning functions are used for calculations that will return values to the calling function.

Passing by value passes a copy of the values to be used for calculations, pass by reference passes a pointer to the variable that allows the called function to use the values stored in those variables in the calling program and alter their contents directly.

Function stubs are a great way to allow the programmer to test the main function or any calling function, prior to beginning to code the function. This allows the programmer to return a known value to provide a better test for the function presently being tested.

End of Lesson Quiz

All functions except the _____ type must have a return statement.

The function call for a _____ function is simply the name of the function followed by the actual parameters.

Use pass by _____ when you want the function to have access to the contents of a variable and allow the called function to change the value contained in that variable.

Function _____ is a technique that allows you to write and test parts of the program without having to have all components ready before testing.

SECTION VI - Random Numbers and Files

Lesson 23
Random Numbers

Objectives:
- Use random numbers in a program.
- Explain upperbound and lowerbound.
- Describe the process to set the random number seed.
- List the steps in creating a random number.

Lesson 23.1 : Random Number - Theory and Use

Many games require random numbers. While an algorithm can be developed to generate a random number, C++, like many other programming languages, offers a function that will generate random numbers for the programmer. In this lesson we will look at how C++ generates a random number.

First, a random number needs a "seed" to generate a random number. The seed is simply a number that changes frequently within the system. Usually, this seed is derived from the system clock. Once the algorithm has the seed it can generate a random number, C++ generates an integer between 0 and 32767.

In the programming languages that have a function to generate the random number, the programmer usually supplies a statement that specifies the lower bound and upper bound numbers for the function to generate random numbers in that required range. In the case of generating a routine that generates six numbers to simulate dice, the lower bound number is one and the upper bound number is a six.

Lesson 23.2 : Coding Random Numbers

In this lesson we will look at how C++ uses the time(), srand() and rand() functions to generate random numbers. First we will need to include two new directives: ctime for the time() function and cstdlib for the rand() and srand() functions.

```
#include<ctime>          // for the time() function
#include<cstdlib>        // for the srand() and rand() functions
```

Three functions will be required in your program. The srand() function generates the seed to insure rand() comes up with a statistically random number. We use the time() function to give us a starting number. The time() function returns the seconds from the system clock as an integer. Without setting the seed the rand() function will always return the same number.

```
srand(time(0));
```

The rand() function returns an integer value between 0 and 32,767. To create a value between 0 and 100 you would use the following statement:

```
rand() % 100;
```

The syntax for the rand() statement to generate random numbers between two values is as follows:

```
(rand() % upperbound) + lowerbound;
```

Here is an example of a program that simulates rolling two dice.

```
// dice.cpp
// Date:
// Author:
// roll two dice

#include<iostream>
#include<ctime>            // for the time() function
#include<cstdlib>          // for the srand() and rand() functions
using namespace std;

int main()
{
        // declare variables
        int die1 = 0;
        int die2 = 0;

        // set the seed
        srand(time(0));

        // roll the first die
        die1 = (rand() % 6 ) + 1;

        // roll the second die
        die2 = (rand() % 6 ) + 1;

        // display the results
        cout << "Die #1: " << die1 << endl;
        cout << "Die #2: " << die2 << endl;
        return 0;
}       // end of main function
```

When we examine the statements that generate the numbers of the roll of the dice we see the following. First, we must have a variable to which the random number will be assigned. Then we invoke the random number function rand() which will return an integer value between 0 and 32767. Then we mod that number (take the remainder of integer division) by the highest number we wish to generate (upperbound). Lastly we add the lowest number we wish to generate (lowerbound).

Lesson 23.3 : USING RANDOM NUMBERS

Random numbers are useful for games of chance like the dice game above. We can also use random numbers for simulations and applications where we go through data and randomly select records from a database. However, the random numbers we generate, while statistically random are more properly called pseudorandom numbers.

When using random numbers in a program, testing becomes even more important. If the range is very large it is quite difficult to test but when you are working with a small range of numbers, make sure each number required is generated. When the range is large make sure that all numbers generated fall within the range specified and you have seen the upperbound and lowerbound numbers. Even this testing is sometimes not sufficient but, make sure, in repeated tests, that the numbers are truly random.

Once again let's look at the required statements and their syntax:

```
// make sure you include these directives
```

```
#include<ctime>            // for the time() function
#include<cstdlib>          // for the srand() and rand() functions

// set the random number seed
srand(time(0));

// get the random number
variablename = (rand() % upperbound) + lowerbound;
```

Include the two required directives.   Use srand() to set the random number seed. This only
needs to be set once in the program. Then the rand() function must have an upperbound and
lowerbound value and the function returns a random number to the variable indicated in the
function call.

Lesson 23.4 SAMPLE PROGRAM

A sample C++ program is shown below. This program generates a random number between 1 and
100 and asks the user to guess the number. As the user guesses a number the computer
compares the guess with the number generated and if the user has guessed a number lower it
responds with an appropriate message. If the number guessed is higher than the number
generated, once again the program responds with an appropriate message. If the user guesses
the number exactly, a message of congratualtions is generated. NOTE: the statement that
generates the random number combines the rand() and srand() functions into one statement.

```
// guess.cpp
// Date:
// Author:

#include<iostream>
#include<ctime>            // for the time() function
#include<cstdlib>          // for the srand() and rand() functions
using namespace std;

int main()
{
      // declare variables
      int guess = 0;
      int gennum = 0;
      bool complete = false;

      // set seed and generate a number
      gennum = (rand() + time(0)) % 100;

      // loop to request a guess and do the comparisons
      while (!complete)
      {
      cout << "Enter an integer between 1 and 100: " << endl;
      cin >> guess;
      // compare and generate a response
      if (guess == gennum)
            {
                  cout << "Correct" << endl;
                  complete = true;
            }
      else
            if (guess > gennum)
                  {
                        cout << "Guess is High" << endl;
```

```
                    cout << "Try again" << endl;
            }
        else
            {
                    cout << "Guess is Low" << endl;
                    cout << "Try again" << endl;
            }
    }     // end while


        return 0;
}      // end of main function
```

Lesson 23.5 Summary

Random numbers have many uses in C++ programming. Perhaps, the most significant use is the gaming industry. To use random numbers in your program you need to include two directives, ctime and stdlib. These two directives contain the three functions required to generate random numbers. The srand() and time() functions generate a random number using the system time. The rand() function generates a random number between the specifed lowerbound (low number) and the upperbound (highest number). The range of numbers that may be generated is in the range of 0 to 32767.

End of Lesson Quiz

The rand() function needs a _____ to generate a random number.

The _____ function generates the seed used to generate a random number.

The rand() function returns an integer between _____ and _____.

Lesson 24
File Input and Output

Objectives:

- Identify sequential files.
- Create code to write to a sequential file.
- Create code to read from a sequential file.
- Create code to add to an existing sequential file.
- Describe sequential file processing.

Lesson 24.1 : Sequential Data Files

Now, let's look at sequential files using C++. First we must sort out some terms used in referencing files.

Fields, records and data files need to be defined and understood.

Field - a single piece of information like a social security number.

Record - one or more related fields about a single subject, a first name, last name and a social security number would compose a RECORD containing three FIELDS.

Data File - a collection of related records, for example one of the records described above for each student in the college.

Sequential files are the most basic of file structures. They are similar to cassette tapes of music where you must listen to each song starting at the beginning of the tape. It is difficult to skip to a specific song as you have to pass the tape from the start to the point the song begins. Sequential files are very easy to create but have limitations. First you can only process in records in the order they are stored. This type of file system is best on small files of 100 records or less. If you create large files, the records are always processed in the order in which they were created on the tape.

We will be working with two types of files, input files which are files that already contain data for input into the processing of the program. We will also work with output files. These are new files that will be created by the program or existing files that will have data added as the result of processing. The operation of adding records to an existing file is called appending records.

When writing a program to process sequential files, the first thing we must remember to do is to see that the include directive for processing sequential files is written into the directives section of the program. This directive is:

```
#include <fstream>
```

The next step is to create an object with a name to refer to the object that reflects the object's function. Will this object be used as Input or Output. Based on the answer to that question we create the object with one of the following statements

```
ifstream objectname; //create an input file object, name objectname assigned
                         to object
ofstream objectname; //create an output file object, name objectname assigned
                         to object
```

The keyword ifstream indicates an input file and the objectname is any name you wish to give to the object. It should follow the rules for creating variable names. The keyword ofstream indicates an output file, and the objectname can be any name, subject to the rules for variable names.

Next we must open the file for use by the program. The open process determines how the file will be opened, for input, for output or for appending records (adding records to the end of an existing file) as well as the location and name of the file.

To open a file use:

```
objectname.open(filename,[mode]);
```

objectname = name of object created in ifstream or ofstream

filename = d:/path/filename.ext the name of the file and if the file is located or is to be created in a directory other than the current directory, you must give the DOS path for the direction to the folder in which you wish to store the file.

mode =   ios::in   input – contains data for processing by the program
               ios::app   append – add records to an existing file
               ios::out   output – create a new file.

It is important to understand that if you open a file with the mode ios::out you will create a new file or if the file already exists you will overwrite any existing data. If you open a file with the mode ios::app you will append records to an existing file or if the file does not exist it will act exactly like ios::out and create a new file by that name in the directory indicated.

Next we must test to find out if the file open was successful. If the file open was not successful we need to warn the operator and take some type of corrective action or cancel the program. We can test to see if the open failed or if the open did not fail. To do this we have some options. We could write instructions like:

Test if open failed:

```
if(objectname.fail() == 1)    OR
if(objectname.fail())
```

If either of these if statements test true, the file did not open and the program should take the appropriate actions

Test if open did NOT fail(open successful)

```
if(objectname.fail()==0)  OR
if(!objectname.fail())
```

If either of these if statements test true, the file opened successfully and processing may continue.

Lesson 24.2 : Getting Input from a File

Reading data from a sequential file is similar to getting data from the common input. In place of the cin keyword, we use the name of the object we gave to the file in the open statement for that file.

```
objectname >> data;
```

When we read data from the keyboard or from a file we use similar statement structure syntax. First the name of the object that will be reading the data, cin or the objectname assigned to a file. Next, the extraction operator " >> " and finally the name of the variable where the the input value will be stored at the end of the instruction.

Data from:
```
        cin >> variablename;          // get data from the keyboard
        inFile >> variablename;       // get data from a sequential file
```

The first statement stores the data entered at the common input into the indicated variable. The second statement takes data from the file opened as inFile and stores the data in the indicated variable.

Lesson 24.3 : Writing Data to a File

Writing data to a sequential file is similar to the common output with the cout statement that we have used so frequently in other lessons. In place of the cout keyword, we use the name of the object we gave to this file in the beginning of our program.

```
        objectname << data << endl;
```

When we write to the screen (common output) or to an output file (new file or append to an existing file) we use the following syntax. First the name of the output object followed by the insertion operator " << " and finally the name of the variable containing the data to be output.

Examples:
```
        outFile << score << endl;

        payOut << wkPay << " " << hours << endl;

        outData << textline << endl;

        studentData << lname << ";" << fname << ";" << socsecnbr << endl;
```

The first example shows the contents of the variable named score and an end of record, written to the object named outFile.

The second example shows the contents of the variable named wkPay, the string literal of one space, the contents of the variable named hours and an end of record, written to the object named payOut.

The third example shows the contents of the variable named textline and an end of record, written to the object named outData.

The last example shows the contents of the variable named lname, a semicolon (;), the contents of the variable fname, another semicolon (;), the contents of the variable named socsecnbr, and an end of record, written to the object named studentData.

Lesson 24.4 : WRITING STRING DATA

Writing variables containing strings or writing string literals to output files are no different than writing them with a cout statement. Pay close attention to how the data is aligned and spaced on the file. Use spaces, delimiters, to make the data usable by the program that will be used to display the file.

```
        outfile << firstname << " " << lastname << endl;
```

This will display the contents of the variable called firstname, a space character, and the contents of the variable lastname and finally the end of line character.

EXAMPLE:
```
        outfile << "Hourly Pay Rate: " << payRate << endl;
```

This will display the string literal "Hourly Pay Rate: ", followed by the contents of the variable payRate and the end of line character. Note the string literal has a space after the colon and before the closing quotation marks. This puts a space between the string literal and the value displayed from the variable payRate.

Lesson 24.5 : IGNORE FUNCTION

THE IGNORE FUNCTION

The ignore function is used to disregard or skip characters entered at the keyboard or from the input file. It is also good for clearing the input buffer after reading strings or char arrays, and must always be used after reading a string from either the keyboard or from file input. NOTE: Once you use the Ignore function in a program in must be used for ALL inputs in the program. Call the function after each input, string, char, numeric, etc.

The Syntax:

```
        cin.ignore([nCount],[,delimChar]);
```

both arguments are optional.
        nCount = number of characters to read and ignore
        delimChar = the delimiting character that stops reading

```
cin.ignore(100);         // skips first 100 character
cin.ignore(100,'A');     // skips 100 character or until the letter 'A' is
                            encountered
```

The example below will allow a voter's name to be entered using the common input and then clears the input buffer.

```
        cin.get(voter.name,25,'\n'); //gets voter name
        cin.ignore(100, '\n');   //discards '\n' from enter key
```

The ignore statement above will examine the cin buffer for up to 100 characters or until it encounters a '\n' character (the character generated by clicking on the enter key).

Lesson 24.6 : PASSING FILES TO FUNCTIONS

Often a function is the best way to process data being read from or written to a file. This is especially true when the same file is processed in several different programs. When a file is passed to a function, as you will note in the examples, it is passed by reference.

The first example illustrates creating a file in a void function named outnum(). The file is declared and opened in the main function, but the void function is used to write records to the file. Examine the program below and carefully note the (1) prototype; (2) declaration and opening of the output file; (3) the function call; and (4) the actual void function.

EXAMPLE:

```cpp
// iofunction1.cpp
// Date:
// Author:

#include<iostream>
#include<fstream>
using namespace std;

void outnum(double num, ostream & out);

int main()
{
        double num = 0;

        ofstream outFile;
        outFile.open("input.txt");

        do
        {
        cout << "Enter a number (0 to quit): ";
        cin >> num;

        outnum(num, outFile);
        } while (num > 0);

        outFile.close();

} // End Main Function

void outnum(double num, ostream & out)
{
        out << num << " " << num << endl;

} // End readnum Function
```

First look in the prototype, the second argument in the void prototype named outnum, is a pass by reference.   Next, in the main function we declare an output file which will be called outFile and then open the actual file "input.txt". The third important point is the function call. The actual parameters are the number being passed to be output to the file and the output file declared as "outFile". Last, we look at the void function outnum(). The formal parameters show the number that is passed (the first argument) and the second argument is the pass by reference of the output file declared as "outFile".

The second example program accepts the file generated in the first program example which we named "input.txt", as an input and then it is read by a void function named readnum() that reads and prints the contents of the file to the common output device.

As in the first example program, it is important to look at (1) the function prototype; (2) the declaration and open of the input file; (3) the function call; and (4) the function itself.

EXAMPLE:

```
// iofunction2.cpp
// Date:
// Author:

#include<iostream>
#include<fstream>
using namespace std;

void readnum(istream & inp);

int main()
{
        ifstream inFile;
        inFile.open("input.txt");
        readnum(inFile);
        cout << "End of Processing" << endl;
}  // End Main Function

void readnum(istream & inp)
{
        int num;
        inp >> num;
        while (num != 0)
        {
                cout << num << endl;
                inp >> num;
        }
}  // End readnum Function
```

The sole argument in the prototype is a pass by reference of the file named "input.txt". The main program opens input.txt as inFile. The function call passes the actual parameter, infile to the void function readnum(). The function readnum() accepts the formal parameter as pass by reference and reads each record, outputting its contents to the common output device.

The last example program puts both file creation and file read in the same program.

EXAMPLE:

```
#include<iostream>
#include<fstream>
using namespace std;

void outnum(double num, ostream & out);
void readnum(istream & inp);

int main()
{
        double num = 0;
        ofstream outFile;
        outFile.open("input.txt");

        do
        {
        cout << "Enter a number (0 to quit): ";
        cin >> num;
```

```
        outnum(num, outFile);
    } while (num > 0);
    outFile.close();

    cout << endl << "Now read the file generated" << endl << endl;
    ifstream inFile;
    inFile.open("input.txt");
    readnum(inFile);
    cout << "End of Processing" << endl;
} // End Main Function

void outnum(double num, ostream & out)
{
    out << num << " " << num << endl;

} // End outnum Function

void readnum(istream & inp)
{
    int num;
    inp >> num;
    while (num != 0)
    {
        cout << num << endl;
        inp >> num;
    }
} // End readnum Function
```

The function to create the file is completed first and the file created is closed. Then the same file is opened as an input file and the contents displayed on the common output device.

Lesson 24.7 : SAMPLE PROGRAM

A sample C++ program is shown below. This program reads a file that contains the student name and the students grades. The program processes the grades to determine an average and then calculates the letter grade. When this process is complete the program will output a new file containing the student name, average grade and letter grade.

INPUT FILE:

```
smith 90 95 79 88 100
jones 77 79 72 81 80
green 58 77 81 80 89
bortz 34 58 61 55 70
chang 100 93 91 100 100
```

PROGRAM:

```
// grades.cpp
// Date:
// Author:

#include <iostream>
#include <fstream>
#include <string>
using namespace std;
```

```cpp
int main()
{
// declare variables
string name;
int g1, g2, g3, g4, g5;
int total;
double avg;
int grade;
char letter;

// create objects
ifstream gradeIn;
ofstream gradeOut;
// open files
gradeIn.open("ClassGrade.txt", ios::in);
if (gradeIn.fail())
    {
    cout << "Input Failed" << endl;
    return 1;
    }
gradeOut.open("FinalGrade.txt", ios::out);
if (gradeOut.Fail())
    {
    cout << "Output Failed" << endl;
    return 1;
    }
// get next input record

gradeIn >> g1 >> g2 >> g3 >> g4 >> g5;
getline(gradeIn, name);

// loop to process data
while (!gradeIn.eof())
{
    total = g1 + g2 + g3 + g4 + g5;
    avg = total / 5;
    grade = static_cast<int>(avg);

    if (grade >= 90) letter = 'A';
    if (grade >= 80 && grade < 90) letter = 'B';
    if (grade >= 70 && grade < 80) letter = 'C';
    if (grade >= 60 && grade < 70) letter = 'D';
    if (grade < 60) letter = 'F';

    // output data to output file
    gradeOut << name << " " << grade << " " << letter << endl;

    // get next input record
    gradeIn >> g1 >> g2 >> g3 >> g4 >> g5;
    getline(gradeIn, name);

}    // end of while loop

// close files
    gradeIn.close();
    gradeOut.close();
    return 0;
}  // end of main function
```

OUTPUT FILE:

```
smith 90 A
jones 78 C
green 77 C
bortz 56 F
chang 97 A
```

Lesson 24.8 Summary

A sequential data file is processed from the first record to the last record. A file consists of records and records consist of fields. For a C++ program to process sequential files, it is necessary to include a directive name fstream. The program must create an object for the file and give it a name. The keyword ifstream is used to create an input file object and ofstream to create an output file object. Then the file must be opened. This step tells the program how to find the file, (name and location) as well as information about how the file should be opened. The file may be opened as an input file, append to an input file or opened as an output file. Then, the program can read/write data to/from the file.

End of Lesson Quiz

A _____ is a single piece of information like a social security number.

_____ files are the most basic of file structures.

When creating a file object name, the keyword _____ indicates an input file.

To add records to an existing file you need to specify the mode as _____.

The _____ function is used to disregard or skip characters entered at the keyboard or from and input file.

SECTION VII - Arrays

Lesson 25
One Dimensional Arrays

Objectives:

- Explain the concept of arrays.
- Declare an array.
- Add data to an array.
- Read data from an array.
- Find the highest value in an array.
- Find the lowest value in an array.

Lesson 25.1 : Introduction to Arrays

You can think of an array as a group of variables with one name. You address and manipulate individual items in this group by using a value referred to as an index.

Arrays can be one dimensional, two dimensional or multi-dimensional. In this lesson we will only examine one dimensional. Arrays are used to give the same variable names to multiple, similar items.

A good example of an array is when we want to store the days of the week. There are seven days in each week and when we want to store the names of the days of the week we could declare seven variables, one for each day. Example: Sunday, Monday, Wednesday, etc.

However, they could all be named something like dayName rather than seven different variable names. Arrays will allow us to name all seven variables dayName and index them by their day number (Sunday = index 0; Monday = index 1; Tuesday = index 2 and so on).

Arrays are used to store data in memory for faster access. The computer accesses memory much faster than disk. So, keeping data like small tables that are accessed frequently, in memory can speed up processing transactions in an application.

Lesson 25.2 : Declaring Arrays

In using an array, the first thing that must be done is to declare that array. Let's look at a problem that may be solved without an array and then with an array to illustrate how much easier it is to use an array for this type of problem.

Example Problem: A shipping company has 4 shipping zones. The zones are numbered 1, 2, 3 and 4. Each shipping zone has a different charge per pound for delivering goods. Zone 1 charge is $1.40 per pound; Zone 2 charge is $1.90 per pound; Zone 3 charge is $2.80 per pound and Zone 4 charge is $3.90 per pound. Let's look at a couple approaches to defining the variables.

We can reserve and initialize four variables each with a different name as follows:

```
float zone1 = 1.40;    // per pound for zone 1
float zone2 = 1.90;    // per pound for zone 2
float zone3 = 2.80;    // per pound for zone 3
float zone4 = 3.90;    // per pound for zone 4
```

This results in four variables created in memory as illustrated in the table below:

Variable Name	Contents
zone1	1.40
zone2	1.90
zone3	2.80
zone4	3.90

Or we can reserve and initialize four variables as an array using the following code to declare the array:

```
float zone(4);
```

This code would declare an array that can hold four variables of the data type float. Then we could assign a value to each member of the array as follows:

```
zone[0] = 1.40;
zone[1] = 1.90;
zone[2] = 2.80;
zone[3] = 3.90;
```

These instructions load each element of the array with its proper value. Note that the first element of the array is addressed as zero (0). This will be explained later in the next lesson.

If we would like to consolidate the five lines of code into one line and initialize the variable as we declare it we can use this line of code:

```
float zone[4] = {float(1.40), float(1.90), float(2.80), float(3.90)};
```

Either method results in four variables created in memory as illustrated in the table below:

Variable Name	Index	Contents
zone	0	1.40
zone	1	1.90
zone	2	2.80
zone	3	3.90

So, we can declare four variables or declare an array of four values. In both cases we are reserving 4 segments of memory each containing a value. At first glance there are little difference in doing it either way. However consider the programming required to access each of the elements using a larger number of elements. Arrays can hold hundreds of variables. The array is declared in the program and may be loaded at declaration or loaded with values from an external file during program execution. The values could be a result of calculations or other processing. This could present a programming nightmare.

Lesson 25.3 : Syntax

No let us look at the syntax to declare an array. The syntax for declaring an array variable is:

```
datatype arrayname[n-Elements] = {initial values};
```

Datatype	Any C++ datatype
Arrayname	Name of the array – same rules as variable names
n-Elements	An integer that represents the number of elements in the array, must be enclosed in square brackets. []
Initial values	Values to initialize any or all elements of the array.

Each element has a unique address composed of the arrayname + the subscript(or index as it is referred to by some). The first element is subscript 0, the second element is subscript 1 and so on. To express the unique variablename for the very first element in an array, you write arrayname[0].

We can use arrays to store data in many different data types. Let's look at some different data types and how they would be initialized:

NUMERIC VARIABLES

```
int num[3] = {0, 0, 0};        // places 0 in each element of the array
int num[3] = {0};              // places 0 in each element of the array
int num[3] = {3, 5, 7};        // initializes the three elements to values

int bigarray[30] = {0};             // zero is put in all elements,
                               good for large arrays

float cost[10] = {(float) 5.2};  // first element is initialized to 5.2 and
                                    the remainder to 0.
```

Some other examples of arrays of other data types are:

```
string State[4]={"DE","MD","PA","VA"};
double Price[6]={double(10.99)};        // first variable is 10.99 all others 0
int areaCode[3]={302,410,215};
```

Arrays of characters were used in older versions of C++ and C to hold strings of data. This use of arrays made handling string data a chore for programmers. C and C++ were not designed with strings of data in mind. One of the more annoying characteristics of strings stored in arrays of type char was that you had to reserve the last element of the array for a null character (\0) that was used to signify the end of the string.

CHAR VARIABLES

```
char item[5] ="";        // all five elements initialized to NULL values
char item[5] = {""};     // all five elements initialized to NULL values


char item[5] = "Book";                 // the array will contain the string "book"
char item[5] = {'B', 'o', 'o', 'k', '\0'};     // the array will contain the string
"book"
char item[4] = {'B', 'o', 'o', 'k'};       // only contains 4 char and is NOT a
                                           // string
```

```
item 1 = B
item 2 = o
item 3 = o
item 4 = k
item 5 = \0 or the null value indicating the end of the string
```

You must always remember to assign a value one position larger than the number of characters in the string to the index portion of the array declaration to insure you have room for the null character. If you do not have enough room to accommodate the null character ('\0'), the string will be truncated. A null character will always be stored in the last position of the string array.

25.4: Manipulating Data in Arrays

We have looked at how to set up an array and initialize it to values. However, an array is more useful than we have yet to discover. In this lesson we will look at how we can let a user enter data into an array from the keyboard, print data out of an array and find data in an array.

To effectively loop through an array we use counter controlled loops. The for loop is an excellent candidate for processing data in an array. The index number in the for loop construct is ideal for indexing through an array. Let's look at some examples where we enter data into an array, print the data out of an array and then find the highest number and lowest number in the array.

The examples are from a solution to the code used to allow the user to enter seven months of sales, print the contents of the array and then find the month with the highest and lowest sales.

```
// input sales data into an array

double sales[7];              // declare the array
int index = 0;                // declare an index

// loop to allow the user to enter 7 values into the array
for (index=0; index < 7; index++)
{
      cout << "Enter the sales for month number " << index + 1 << " ";
      cin >> sales[index];
}

// printing data from an array

// loop to print the seven values entered in the order they were entered
for (index=0; index < 7; index++)
{
cout << "Sales for month " << index + 1 << " was " << sales[index];
      cout << endl;
}

// finding data in an array (finds largest and smallest values):

int hivalue = 0;         // declare a variable to store highest value.
int lovalue = 0;         // declare a variable to store lowest value.

// loop to find the highest and lowest values
for (index=0; index < 7; index++)
{
      if (sales[hivalue] < sales[index])
            hivalue = index;
      if (sales[lovalue] > sales[index])
```

```
            lovalue = index;
      }

      // display the highest and lowest values
      cout << "Day " << hivalue + 1 << " Highest. ";
      cout << " Sales were $" << sales[hivalue] << endl;
      cout << "Day " << lovalue + 1 << " Lowest. ";
      cout << " Sales were $" << sales[lovalue] << endl;
```

Note that in all of the examples we add one to the index value when we display the number that corresponds to the month. If we did not do that, we would display a 0 for Sunday and an 6 for Saturday and that would be confusing to the one who inputs the data or reads the report.

Look carefully at the loop that finds the highest and lowest values. This process sounds so intimidating but in code it is actually very simple. First, we set up a variable to hold the highest value and one to hold the lowest value and initialize them to zero. Then a loop to go through all twelve values and compare to both the highest and lowest values. When a value higher than the current highest value is found the index for the new high value is stored in the appropriate variable. When a value lower than the current lowest value is found the index for the new low value is stored in the appropriate variable. At the end of this process, after all items in the array have been examined, the variable for the high value contains the index to the highest value and the variable for the lowest value contains the index to the lowest value in the array.

Lesson 25.5 SAMPLE PROGRAM

A sample C++ program is shown below. This is the entire program that allows for the entry of twelve months rainfall, prints the twelve months data and then the highest rainfall month and the lowest rainfall month. The program also provides the total rainfall for the year and the average rainfall for the year.

```
// rainfall.cpp
// Date:
// Author:
#include<iostream>
using namespace std;

int main()
{
      //declare variables
      double rainfall[12];
      int index = 0;
      int hivalue = 0;
      int lovalue = 0;
      double sumrainfall = 0.0;
      double avgrain = 0.0;

      // get twelve months of rainfall and total
      for (index=0; index < 12; index++)
      {
            cout << "Enter the rainfall for month number " << index + 1 << " ";
            cin >> rainfall[index];
            sumrainfall += rainfall[index];
      }

      // calculate the average rainfall
      avgrain = sumrainfall / 12.0;

      // find the index of the highest and lowest months
```

```
        for (index=1; index < 12; index++)
        {
                if (rainfall[hivalue] < rainfall[index])
                        hivalue = index;
                if (rainfall[lovalue] > rainfall[index])
                        lovalue = index;
        }

        // display array contents, highest, lowest, total and average
        // rainfall amounts
        for (index=0; index < 12; index++)
        {
        cout << "Rainfall for month " << index + 1 << " was " << rainfall[index];
                cout << endl;
        }
        cout << endl;
        cout << "Month " << hivalue + 1 << " Highest. ";
        cout << " Amount was " << rainfall[hivalue] << endl;
        cout << "Month " << lovalue + 1 << " Lowest. ";
        cout << " Amount was " << rainfall[lovalue] << endl;
        cout << "Total Rainfall: " << sumrainfall;
        cout << endl;
        cout << "Average Rainfall: " << avgrain;
        cout << endl;
        return 0;
}
```

OUTPUT SAMPLE: (you should make up values for each month for data entry)

```
        Rainfall for month 1 was 0.0
        Rainfall for month 2 was 0.0
        Rainfall for month 3 was 0.0
        Rainfall for month 4 was 0.0
        Rainfall for month 5 was 0.0
        Rainfall for month 6 was 0.0
        Rainfall for month 7 was 0.0
        Rainfall for month 8 was 0.0
        Rainfall for month 9 was 0.0
        Rainfall for month 10 was 0.0
        Rainfall for month 11 was 0.0
        Rainfall for month 12 was 0.0
        Month 1 Highest.  Amount was 0.0
        Month 2 Lowest.  Amount was 0.0
        Total Rainfall: 0.0
        Average Rainfall: 0.0
```

Lesson 25.6 Summary

An array is a great way to store lists of data. The data is all the same data type and is referred to by the array name plus the index number of the position of the requested data in the array. Think of an array in terms of a carton that holds a dozen eggs. There are twelve little compartments that each holds one egg. We could refer to the egg in each compartment as egg[0], egg[1], through egg[11] as each compartment holds a like object (an egg).

A character array must be declared and have one more element than needed as an array always ends with a null character ('\0'). If an array is too small to hold the data given to it, data will be truncated. The for loop is one of the best ways to manipulate an array. Use it to load the array, modify elements of the array, display contents of the array, etc.

End of Lesson Quiz

_____ are used to give the same variable name to multiple, similar items.

Each element of the array has a unique address, composed of the array name + the _____.

The first element of an array is subscript _____.

Lesson 26
Parallel Arrays

Objectives:

- Explain the concept of parallel arrays.
- Declare parallel arrays.
- Display data from parallel arrays.
- Put data into parallel arrays.
- Manipulate data in parallel arrays.

Lesson 26.1 Parallel Arrays

In the last chapter we learned about one-dimensional arrays and how they are used to store data. The next step is to learn how we can use two or more of these arrays to store multiple pieces of related data of same or different data types.

The concept of parallel arrays is to use multiple one-dimensional arrays to store data. The first element in each array are all related, the second element in each array are related and so on. Each array will have the same number of elements. While all elements of an array must be of the same data type, with parallel arrays each array can be a different data type.

We can construct a series of parallel arrays to keep track of some information about the students in our class. Array number one will hold the student number and array number two will hold the name of the student. Two different facts, two different data types all about the same student. Later we will add some additional facts we need to store about each student.

Our arrays might look something like this in the computer memory:

Array #1	Array #2	Index #
studentId	studentName	x
1234	John Dough	0
2345	Jim Smith	1
3456	Ann Reyes	2
4567	Jack Wright	3

The code to declare these arrays is:

```
int studentid[4];
string studentname[4];
```

The student id in the first element of the first array corresponds to the first element in the second array. This means that studentid 1234 belongs to Jane Dough and studentid 2345 belongs to Jim Smith and so on. We refer to information about Jane Dough using studentid[0] and studentname[0]. Information about Jim Smith is found at studentid[1] and studentname[1].

Look at the code statement below and using the table we show in the beginning of this lesson, what will be printed?

```
int studentid[4] = {1234, 2345, 3456, 4567};
string studentname[4] = {"{Jane Dough", "Jim Smith", "Ann Reyes", "Jack
Wright"};
```

```
int x = 0;

for (x=0; x<4; x++)
{
        cout << "Student: " << studentid[x];
        cout << " " << studentname[x] << endl;
}
```

The output would look like this:

```
Student: 1234 Jane Dough
Student: 2345 Jim Smith
Student: 3456 Ann Reyes
Student: 4567 Jack Wright
```

Let's examine the code we generated to print out the studentid that corresponds to the matching studentname. First, we start with a simple FOR loop that starts at zero and stops when the value of x reaches 4. This will be sufficient to output all four elements in each of the parallel arrays. NOTE: Each array must have EXACTLY the same number of elements but, each array need not be the same data type.

The loop consists of two cout instructions. One to output the string literal "Student: " to the common output device and output the studentid which addresses one of the elements of array one. The second cout statement outputs a blank space followed by the studentname which addresses the corresponding element in array two. Each time through the loop the value of x which started at 0, will be incremented by one until it reaches 4 and then it will exit the loop. As the value of x changes each time through the loop, it addresses a different set of data in each array. As long as the data matches, the output will be correct. Again, there must be the same number of elements in each array but each array need not be the same data type.

Lesson 26.2 Using Parallel Arrays

In lesson one we looked at two parallel arrays. Two arrays is not a limitation. We may have as many parallel arrays as it takes to hold the data required. We will continue to build on the arrays we began in the first lesson.

Since we can now store studentid and studentname, we need to expand the parallel array structure to include three arrays to hold the quiz grades for the semester. Our series of parallel arrays will now look like this:

```
int studentid[4] = {1234, 2345, 3456, 4567};
string studentname[4] = {"{Jane Dough", "Jim Smith", "Ann Reyes", "Jack
Wright"};
int q1[4] = {0};  // quiz grade one
int q2[4] = {0};     // quiz grade two
int q3[4] = {0};     // quiz grade three
```

We now need to put the quiz grades into the computer.

```
int x = 0;
for (x=0; x<4; x++)
{
        cout << "Enter Quiz Grade 1: ";
        cin >> q1[x];
        cout << "Enter Quiz Grade 2: ";
        cin >> q2[x];
        cout << "Enter Quiz Grade 3: ";
```

```
                cin >> q3[x];
        }
```

To access the student data, we can extend the code we used for entering data into the two parallel arrays.

```
        for (x=0; x<4; x++)
        {
                cout << "Student: " << studentid[x];
                cout << " " << studentname[x];
                cout << " " << q1[x] << " " << q2[x];
                cout << " " << q3[x] << endl;
        }
```

As you can see in the last two examples, we can step through the arrays using a for loop and using the index value for the for loop to access each row in the array.

This begins to illustrate the power of parallel arrays and the for loop structure. Once again, as is constant in all programming, a little planning can save a lot of work.

Another bonus with parallel arrays is that the arrays can be different data types. So far, in our example we have used two different data types, string and integer. In the next lesson we will add two additional data types, double and char and learn how to do math on the arrays and make decisions based on array contents.

Lesson 26.3 Calculations in Parallel Arrays

In this lesson we learn how to do more than put data in and out of arrays. Quite often it is necessary to manipulate that data. So, back to our example we have been using throughout this chapter. We need to add some arrays to our list. One to store the calculated average of the three courses and one to hold the letter grade for the course. An A for an average of 90 to 100, a B for an average of 80 to 89, a C for an average of 70 to 79, a D for an average of 60 to 69 and an F for below 60.

First, we need to declare two more arrays to add to our list:

```
        double avg[4] = {0};
        char grade[4];
```

Then we need to add some code to calculate the average and convert it to a letter grade storing the average in the avg array and the letter grade in the grade array.

```
        for (x=0;  x<4; x++)
        {
                avg[x] = (q1[x] + q2[x] + q3[x]) / 3;
                if (avg[x] >= 90)
                        grade[x] = 'A';
                else if (avg[x] >= 80)
                        grade[x] = 'B';
                else if (avg[x] >=70)
                        grade[x] = 'C';
                else if (avg[x] >= 60)
                        grade[x] = 'D';
                else if (avg[x] < 60)
                        grade[x] = 'F';
        }
```

Now we have a program that declares parallel arrays, puts data into the array, calculates a value using array data storing the answer in the array, and add to the array based on the values of the contents in another parallel array.

Lesson 26.4 Sample Program

This is a program that has three parallel arrays, one for student id one for student name and one for the sum of four quiz grades. The program asks the user to enter, for each student, four quiz grade and then prints the student id, the student name and the average of the four quiz grades. The program terminates after all four students have been processed and printed.

```cpp
// parallel.cpp
// Date:
// Author:
// using parallel arrays

#include<iostream>
#include<iomanip>
using namespace std;

int main()
{
    // declare variables
    int studentid[4] = {1234, 2345, 3456, 4567};
    string studentname[4] = {"{Jane Dough", "Jim Smith", "Ann Reyes",
        "Jack Wright"};
    int q = 0;                  // quiz grade
    int sumq[4] = {0};          // array for quiz grades
    int index = 0;              // index used in for loops

    // loop to enter quiz grades
    for (index = 0; index < 4; index++)
    {
        cout << "Enter grade " << index + 1 << "for student ";
        cout << studentid[index] << "   " << studentname[index];
        cout << endl;
        cin >> q;
        sumq[index] += q
    }

    // loop to print average of quiz grades
    for (index = 0; index < 4; index++)
    {
        cout << "Average Quiz grade for student: " << studentid[index];
        cout << "   " << studentname[index] << " is ";
        cout << sumq[index] / 4 << endl;
    }

    return 0;
}
```

OUTPUT:
```
Average Quiz grade for student 1234 Jane Dough is 0000.00
Average Quiz grade for student 2345 Jim Smith is 0000.00
Average Quiz grade for student 3456 Ann Reyes is 0000.00
Average Quiz grade for student 4567 Jack Wright is 0000.00
```

Lesson 26.5 Summary

Parallel arrays allow the programmer to use groups of one dimensional arrays to store several groups of related data in arrays. The data in the arrays are ordered where the data in the first element of each array are related, the second element of each array are related and so on. All of the operations that can be done on a one-dimensional array can be done on parallel arrays.

End of Lesson Quiz

The concept of _____ _____ is to use multiple one-dimensional arrays to store data.

All elements of an array must be of the same _____ _____.

Each array in a parallel array can be of _____ data types.

Lesson 27
Multi-Dimensional Arrays

Objectives:

- Explain the concept of multi-dimensional arrays.
- Declare a two-dimensional array.
- Display data from a two-dimensional array.
- Put data into a two-dimensional array.
- Manipulate data in a two-dimensional array.

Lesson 27.1 Two-Dimensional Arrays

In our lessons on one-dimensional arrays and parallel arrays, we learned how to declare, initialize, manipulate and display array contents in a one-dimensional array.

A one-dimensional array is similar to a list of items of the same data type. A two-dimensional array is more like a spreadsheet. It consists of rows and columns of data. The biggest constraint is that all of the data in the rows and columns must be of the same data type. If you declare the array as type integer, all of the elements of the array will store only integer data.

The syntax for a two-dimensional array is:

```
datatype     varname[rowindex][columnindex];
```

Now to put that into C++ code, to declare a variable of 3 rows and 3 columns, we would declare the array as follows:

```
double shipcust[3][3];
```

The resultant array would look like this:

shipcust		[0]	[1]	[2]
	[0]			
	[1]			
	[2]			

Note the array has three columns and three rows of variables to store data of data type double. The statement cout << shipcost[1][2]; would refer to the data in the cell in row 1 column 2. Again, like one-dimensional arrays, the indexing of two-dimensional arrays is zero based.

Lesson 27.2 Using Two-Dimensional Arrays

Let's put some values in our array:

shipcust		[0]	[1]	[2]
	[0]	1.23	2.34	3.45
	[1]	1.59	2.65	3.71
	[2]	1.89	2.92	3.99

It is time to write some code that will declare a two-dimensional array named shipcust, initialize the array to values and using a nested for loop, print out the data in the array.

```
double shipcost[3][3] = {      {1.23, 2.34, 3.45},
                               {1.59, 2.65, 3.71},
                               {1.89, 2.92, 3.99}   };
int x = 0;
int z = 0;

for (x=0; x<3; x++)
{
        for (z=0; z<3; z++)
        {
        cout << "Zone:           " << z << endl;
        cout << "Weight Class:   " << x << endl;
        cout << "Cost:           " << shipcost[x][z] << endl;
        }
}
```

The trickiest part to understand in this code segment is the nested for loops. The outer loop controls the rows and the inner loop controls the columns within each row. The first time through the outer loop the inner loop prints all the columns in row zero, the second time through the outer loop the inner loop prints all of the columns in row one, and the third time through the outer loop the inner loop prints all of the columns in row two.

Lesson 27.3 Manipulating Two-Dimensional Arrays

Manipulating data using two-dimensional arrays, is no different than manipulating data in one-dimensional arrays. Using our example of the shipping costs, we will have a user enter the zone and the weight for all of the packages they are shipping and when they have entered all of the packages the program will give them a total cost for shipping those packages.

```
double shipcost[3][3] = {      {1.23, 2.34, 3.45},
                               {1.59, 2.65, 3.71},
                               {1.89, 2.92, 3.99}   };
int x = 0;
int z = 0;
char response = 'Y';
double total = 0.0;

while (response = 'Y')
{
        cout << "Enter package weight class(1, 2, or 3) " << endl;
        cout << "1 = less than 1 pound" << endl;
        cout << "2 = 1 pound to 5 pounds" << endl;
        cout << "3 = over 5 pounds" << endl;
        cin >> x;
        cout << "Enter shipping zone: ";
        cin >> z;
        total = total + shipcost[x][z];
        cout << "Do you have another package Y or N ? ";
        cin >> response;
}
cout << "Total Shipping Cost = " << total << endl;
```

In this example the user enters the number of the row that corresponds to the weight of the package followed by the shipping zone of the package destination.

Lesson 27.4 Sample Program

This is a program that has a two-dimensional array that holds the daily temperature for each of four weeks. The program reads each weeks tempeatures, totals them and then displays the average tempeature for that week.

```cpp
// twodim.cpp
// Date:
// Author:
// using two-dimensional arrays

#include<iostream>
#include<iomanip>
using namespace std;

int main()
{
      // declare variables
      int weektemp[4][7] = {  {87, 84, 82, 82, 80, 82, 81},
                              {80, 84, 85, 85, 84, 84, 85},
                              (85, 85, 87, 87, 86, 87, 87),
                              {87, 88, 91, 94, 92, 96, 94}  };
      int x = 0;
      int z = 0;
      int total = 0;

      // calculate the average for each week and print

      for (x=0; x<4; x++)
      {
            for (z=0; z<7; z++)
            {
                  total = total = weektemp[x][z];
            }
            cout << "Average Temperature for week " << z;
            cout << " is " << total/7 << endl;
            total = 0;
      }
   return 0;
   }
```

```
OUTPUT:
   Average Temperature for week 1 is 82.57
   Average Temperature for week 2 is 83.86
   Average Temperature for week 3 is 86.29
   Average Temperature for week 4 is 91.71
```

Lesson 27.5 Summary

A two-dimensional array is similar to a spreadsheet. It consists of rows and columns that store data of the same data type. A good understanding of nested loops in necessary to effectively process data in two-dimensional arrays.

End of Lesson Quiz

A two-dimensional array is like a _____.

The first subscript indicates the _____ and the second subscript indicates the _____.

All elements of a two-dimensional array must all be the _____ data type.

Lesson 28
Arrays and Functions

Objectives:

- Pass an array to a void function.
- Pass an array to a value returning function.
- Explain why passing an array to a function is necessary.
- Code the function prototype.
- Code the function header.
- Code the function call.

Lesson 28.1 Arrays and Functions

Now we move on to using arrays in functions. Many times there are tasks that we perform using arrays that are done in several programs or are required several times in the same program. It is nice to have a function that you can use that will do that for you that you can pull out of your bag of tricks that save you time and work and best of all less typing.

The important thing to remember when we pass an array to a function, we only pass a pointer to the array to the function. This is pass by reference rather than pass by value. The function works with the actual data in the array rather than a copy of the values. So, if you change an array value in a function, it changes the array value in the calling function not a copy.

We declare the array in the main function just as we learned in the past three lessons. That remains the same. However, when we declare our function prototype and function header, it may look something like this:

Syntax:

```
void procedurename(int arrayname[]);
```

Example:

```
void printarray(int avg[]);    // function prototype

void printarray(int avg[])     // function header
```

Note we do not have to put a value in the square brackets of the function prototype or the function header. Also, the function prototype ends in a semicolon where the function header must not have a semicolon at the end.

Lesson 28.2 Passing an array to a void function.

We are going to build a function that we can use to print the contents of ANY one-dimensional array regardless of size. The only restriction is that the values in this array are all of the data type double. Our function will require two arguments, the array and the length of the array. We will do our first function to print out an array of the data type type double. First we will look at the function. Our function will look like this:

```
void printdoublearray(double arrayin[], int len)
{
```

```
        for (int x=0; x<len; x++)
        {
                cout << arrayin[x] << endl;
        }
}
```

This function will work for any array that is type double and the length of the array can be determined. Obviously you could build a function for each of the data types and use them as needed.

When we call the function printdouble array to use the array named arrayin that has six elements, the function call must be in the format:

```
// declare an array
arrayin[6];

// the function call passes the array
// and the length of the array
printdoublearray(arrayin, 6);
```

In the arguments for the function call we only need to give the name of the array, without the square brackets. For the second argument we are giving a value of 6, this could also be a variable containing the length of the array.

Lesson 28.3 Using the function in a program.

Now we will demonstrate how to use our new function to print the values from an array in a main program.

```
// printarray.cpp
// Date:
// Author:
// This demonstrates using the function printdoublearray

#include<iostream>
using namespace std;

void printdouble(double arrayin[], int len);

int main()
{
        double rainfall[4] = {1.23, 2.34, 3.45, 4.56};
        double avgrain[3] = {12.34, 23.45, 34.56};
        int x = 0

        cout << "DAILY RAINFALL" << endl;
        printdoublearray(rainfall, 4);
        cout << "AVERAGE" << endl;
        printdoublearray(avgrain, 3);
return 0;
}    / end of main function

// this is the function
void printdoublearray(double arrayin[], int len)
{
        for (int x=0; x<len; x++)
        {
                cout << arrayin[x] << endl;
```

```
                }
        }
```

Note how we use the same function to print both arrays. This is the power of functions, the ability to reuse code. This must be a consideration when designing the initial function. If you are going to reuse a function, you must consider this when designing the function.

Lesson 28.4 Function call

In the above example we have two function calls:

```
        printdoublearray(rainfall, 4);
        printdoublearray(avgrain, 3);
```

This is the code in your program that transfers control to the function. For a void function, the name of the function followed by open parenthesis, name of the array to be passed, the length of the array, and a close parenthesis followed by the semicolon.

Lesson 28.5 Passing an array to a value returning function.

There is not a lot of difference in passing an array to a value returning function. Remember, the array is being passed not a copy of the array. So, whatever changes are made in the function will be made to the original array data.

```
        // loadarray.cpp
        // Date:
        // Author:
        // This demonstrates using a function to initialize an array

        #include<iostream>
        using namespace std;

        double avgrain(double arrayin[], int len);   //prototype

        int main()
        {
                double rainfall[4] = {1.23, 2.34, 3.45, 4.56};
                int x = 0;
                double avg = 0.0;

                avg = avgrain(rainfall, 4);      // function call

                cout << "Average Rainfall = " << avg << endl;
        return 0;
        } // end of main function
        // this is the value returning function.
        double avgrain(double arrayin[], int len)
        {
        double rainavg = 0.0;
        for (int x=0; x<len; x++)
        {
                rainavg += arrayin[x];
        }
        return rainavg / len;
        } // end of function avgrain
```

Note the differences in the function prototype, function call and function header. First, in the prototype and header, the word void is replaced by the datatype double. This is the datatype that will be returned by the function. Since the function is returning a value, the function call must be able to provide storage for the returned value.

So, the big difference is in the function call. Note that the function call is to the right of the assignment operator (=) and to the left is reference to a variable that can store data of the datatype double. This is where the value returned from the function will be stored.

Lesson 28.6 Sample Program

This is a program that has two arrays and two functions, one function allows the entry of rainfall values for each of twelve months and calculates the average rainfall for the year and a second function that prints the twelve months rainfalls and the average rainfall for the year. The main function declares an array to hold twelve values and a variable to hold the average rainfall returned from the value returning function, rainfall. It also has two instructions both are function calls. The first calls the function rainfall that allows the user to enter the twelve values to complete the array and then calculates the average rainfall for the values entered. The second function call calls the void function which simply prints the twelve months rainfall and then at the end, prints the calculated average.

```
// funcarray.cpp
// Date:
// Author:
// using arrays in functions


#include<iostream>
#include<iomanip>
using namespace std;

// function prototypes
double rainfall(double rainarray[], int len);
void printrain(double rainarray[], int len, double avgrain);

// declare constants
const int len12 = 12;

int main()
{
     // declare variables
     double rainarray[12];
     double avgrain = 0.0;

     // call the rainfall function
     avgrain = rainfall(rainarray, len12);

     // call the printrain function
     printrain(rainarray, len12, avgrain);

     return 0;
} // end of main function
```

```
// value returning function
double rainfall(double rainarray[], int len)
{
double totalrain = 0;
for (int i = 0; i<len; i++)
{
      cout << "Enter rainfall for month " << i+1 << ": ";
      cin >> rainarray[i};
      totalrain += rainarray[i];
}
return totalrain / len;

} // end of function rainfall

// void function to print the array
void printrain(double rainarray[], int len, double avgrain)
{
for (int i=0; i<len; i++)
{
      cout << "Rainfall for month " << i+1 << ": ";
      cout << rainarray[i] << endl;
}
cout << "Average Rainfall for the year: " << avgrain << endl;
} // end of function printrain
```

Lesson 28.7 Summary

Programmers quickly recognize the value of functions. For common problems or tasks write and test once and then use in other programs. For large programs, split the work with others and bring them all together at the end. Whatever you think of functions now, they are a most valuable concept for any programming language. Mastery of functions is essential to the professional programmer. Knowing how to pass arrays to functions is key in using functions. As we have discovered in the past few lessons, arrays are valuable tools in programming. So, as we increase the use of arrays in our programs, it becomes necessary to learn how to pass arrays to functions.

End of Lesson Quiz

When you pass an array to a function, you only pass a _____.

You do not have to put a value in the square brackets in the function _____ or _____.

The power of functions is the ability to _____ _____.

SECTION VIII - Advanced Concepts

Lesson 29
User Defined Data Types (enum)

Objectives:

- Explain the concept of enumerated data types.
- Create a user defined data type.
- Use enum within a program.
- Compare user defined data types.
- Work with enumerator values.

Lesson 29.1 Enumerated data types

An enumerated data type (enum) is a programmer-defined data type. The new data type consists of values (also called enumerators), that represent integer constants. The programmer can create a data type by using the key word enum, a type name, followed by a list of identifiers enclosed in curly braces separated by commas. The type name then becomes a reference to a new data type called an "enumerated data type". This new data type will be able to be used for variables that can hold the values designated for this new data type.

SYNTAX:

```
enum typename {one or more values [enumerators]};
```

EXAMPLES:

```
enum day {MON, TUE, WED, THU, FRI, SAT, SUN};
enum dept {SALES, PRODUCTION, ADMINISTRATION, ACCOUNTING};
```

The enumerators are NOT enclosed in quotes (single or double), they are NOT strings, they are identifiers. All enumerators must be legal C++ identifiers.

Lesson 29.2 Using the enumerated data type

Now that we know how to create an enum data type, we can now use this new data type in our program. The new data type can be used to declare a variable that will accept values by the rules defined within the list. We use this data type just as we would use any other data type studied to date.

```
day dayofweek;
dept AcmeDept = PRODUCTION;
```

Once a variable named dayofweek, with the data type day has been declared, we can assign any of the designated enumerators to the variable of that data type. The only values that the new data type will accept, are those that have been assigned (the enumerators) to that data type.

```
dayofweek = FRI;
AcmeDept = SALES;
```

Now let's examine the question, exactly what are these enumerators? When we set up the enum, the compiler assigns an integer value to each enumerator beginning with zero (0). Using the day enum the following code will demonstrate how the enum is handled by the computer.

```
cout << MON << ", " << TUE << ", " << WED << ", "
     << THU << ", " << FRI << ", " << SAT << ", "
     << SUN << endl;
```

The output will look like this:

0, 1, 2, 3, 4, 5, 6, 7

This is a most important concept to understand when you need to compare enumerator values. The enumerator value is assigned a numeric value beginning with 0.

Lesson 29.3 Working with Enumerator Values

In the last lesson we closed by talking about how enumerators are assigned values beginning with zero by the compiler. Let's look at how we can compare enumerator values.

Comparisons may be done using the relational operators. Using the day data type, the following comparison results in a value of TRUE.

```
WED > TUE
```

WED has a value of 2 and TUE has a value of 1 therefore since 2 is greater than 1 the evaluation results in TRUE.

Using the dept data type the following comparison results in an evaluation of FALSE.

```
SALES > ACCOUNTING
```

In this example SALES has an integer value of 0 and ACCOUNTING has an integer value of 3. The comparison of 0 > 3 results in FALSE.

Looking at a couple of examples using the comparisons in actual code.

EXAMPLE:

```cpp
// enumcompare1.cpp
// Date:
// Author:
#include<iostream>
using namespace std;

enum dept {SALES, PRODUCTION, ADMINISTRATION, ACCOUNTING};
int main()
{
    dept AcmeDept;

    AcmeDept = ADMINISTRATION;

    if (AcmeDept > SALES)
        cout << AcmeDept << endl;
    else
        cout << SALES << endl;

    cout << AcmeDept << endl << endl;
    cout << PRODUCTION << endl << endl;

    return 0;
} // end of main function
```

The output of this program:

    2
    2

    1
    Press any key to continue...

If we change the comparison in the if statement to a < (less than) we get different results.

EXAMPLE

```
// enumcompare2.cpp
// Date:
// Author:
#include<iostream>
using namespace std;

enum dept {SALES, PRODUCTION, ADMINISTRATION, ACCOUNTING};
int main()
{
        dept AcmeDept;

        AcmeDept = ADMINISTRATION;

        if (AcmeDept < SALES)
                cout << AcmeDept << endl;
        else
                cout << SALES << endl;

        cout << AcmeDept << endl << endl;
        cout << PRODUCTION << endl << endl;

        return 0;
} // end of main function
```

The output of this program will look like this:

    0
    2

    1
    Press any key to continue...

Other examples of using these evaluations within our programs to make decisions or use in repetition statements.

```
                If (WED > TUE)
                {
                        cout << "WED is greater than TUE" << endl;
                }

                int count = 0;
                while (count <= SUN)
                {
                        cout << count << ", ";
                        count++;
                }

                If (SALES == 0)
```

```
        {
                cout << "Department 0 is SALES" << endl;
        }
```

Yes, this means that you can compare enumerators to integer values.

Now, let's put what we have learned so far, into a small program.

```
#include <iostream>
using namespace std;

enum day {MON, TUE, WED, THU, FRI, SAT, SUN};
int main()
{

// declare variables
int count = 0;

while (count <= SUN)
{
        cout << count << ", ";
        count++;
}
return 0;
}
```

In this example the enum values are used as a comparison value to determine when the loop should complete.

Lesson 29.4 Using enumerated data types as values

We know that the enumerators are stored in memory as integers. Does that mean that we can add integer values to an enum data type? Examine the line of code:

```
dayofweek = 5;
```

Code written like this will NOT work! It will give an error message that it cannot convert an integer to the data type day. However, the good news is that we really can do this operation, we simply must cast the integer. The proper code is:

```
dayofweek = static_cast<day>(5);
```

This is the equivalent to the instruction:

```
dayofweek = SAT;
```

Now, can we directly assign an enumerator to an integer value? The answer is a great big YES.

```
enum day {MON, TUE, WED, THU, FRI, SAT, SUN};
int count;
count = SUN;
cout << count << endl;
```

When this code is executed, it will display a 6.

```
#include <iostream>
```

```
using namespace std;

enum day {MON, TUE, WED, THU, FRI, SAT, SUN};

int main()
{
    int count = 0;
    for (count=0; count <=SUN; count++)
    {
        cout << static_cast<day>(count) << endl;
    }
return 0;
}
```

This program should display a list of the three character days of the week. Note the use of static_cast to convert the number to the corresponding day of the week in the enum day sequence.

Lesson 29.5 Enum and the switch statement

The enum has many different uses in C++ programming. This lesson will illustrate some additional ways we can use the enum. For our array of AcmeDept we set up a SWITCH statement to print out the full names of the various departments.

```
enum dept {SALES, PRODUCTION, ADMINISTRATION, ACCOUNTING};

 dept AcmeDept;

switch(AcmeDept)
{
        case SALES              :cout << "Acme Sales Dept.";
                                 break;
        case PRODUCTION         :cout << "Acme Production Dept.";
                                 break;
        case ADMINISTRATION     :cout << "Acme Administration Dept.";
                                 break;
        case ACCOUNTING         :cout << "Acme Accounting Dept.";
                                 break;
}
```

The default for enum is to assign the identifiers integer values beginning with zero. Perhaps in our dept example, Acme already has assigned department numbers. This is how we can make the computer assign these existing numbers to the various departments.

```
enum dept {SALES = 110, PRODUCTION = 120, ADMINISTRATION = 130,
           ACCOUNTING = 140);
```

So, rather than the identifiers of dept assigned as 0, 1, 2, 3 they are assigned the values 110, 120, 130, 140. Let's do a program to illustrate this.

```
#include <iostream>
using namespace std;

enum dept {SALES = 110, PRODUCTION = 120, ADMINISTRATION = 130,
           ACCOUNTING = 140};

int main()
{
```

```cpp
      // declare variables
      int AcmeDept = 0;

      // enter department number
      cout << "Select a Department Number (110, 120, 130, or 140): ";
      cin >> AcmeDept;

      // switch statement
      switch(AcmeDept)
      {
            case SALES              :cout << "Dept. # " << AcmeDept;
                                     cout << " is Acme Sales Dept.";
                                      break;
            case PRODUCTION         :cout << "Dept. # " << AcmeDept;
                                     cout << " is Acme Production Dept.";
                                      break;
            case ADMINISTRATION     :cout << "Dept. # " << AcmeDept;
                                     cout << " is Acme Administration Dept.";
                                      break;
            case ACCOUNTING         :cout << "Dept. # " << AcmeDept;
                                     cout << " is Acme Accounting Dept.";
                                     break;
      }
      cout << endl;
      return 0;
      }
```

Lesson 29.6 Some last thoughts on enumerated data types

Some additional thoughts on enums. First, identifiers are just like variable names, named constants, and function names and must adhere to the same rules. Also, they must be unique within their scope. If they are not unique, an error message will be generated.

```cpp
            enum students {Doe, Smith, Carr};
            enum faculty {Able, Baker, Smith};
```

Since the name "Smith" occurs in both enums, this will generate an error message.

Second, you may declare enumerated data types and define one or more variables in the same statement.

```cpp
            enum job {PROGRAMMER, ANALYST, OPERATOR} myjobs;
                      or
            enum job {PROGRAMMER, ANALYST, OPERATOR} myjob, yourjobs;
```

Lesson 29.7 Sample Program

This program asks the user to enter a student number between 1 and 8. The switch statement examines this number and based on a compare to an enum value in the enumerated data type called student, displays that student's grade point average.

```cpp
      // enum.cpp
      // Date:
      // Author:
```

```cpp
#include <iostream>
using namespace std;

enum student {Sam = 1, Ed, Sue, Mike, Matt, Jane, Joe, Sally};
// Sam will have the value of 1 and Ed through Sally values 2 - 8

int main()
{
// declare variables
int nbr = 0;
// Get Student Number from the user
cout << "Enter Student Number (1 to 8): ";
cin >> nbr;

// Display choice based on value entered
switch (nbr)
{
      case Sam   :      cout << "\nSam's GPA is 3.54" << endl;
                        break;
      case Ed    :      cout << "\nEd's GPA is 2.21" << endl;
                        break;
      case Sue   :      cout << "\nSue's GPA is 3.40" << endl;
                        break;
      case Mike  :      cout << "\nMike's GPA is 4.00" << endl;
                        break;
      case Matt  :      cout << "\nMatt's GPA is 4.00" << endl;
                        break;
      case Jane  :      cout << "\nJane's GPA is 2.25" << endl;
                        break;
      case Joe   :      cout << "\nJoe's GPA is 3.09" << endl;
                        break;
      case Sally :      cout << "\nSally's GPA is 4,00" << endl;
                        break;
      default    :      cout << "\nInvalid Student Number" << endl;
} // end of switch statement
return 0;
} // end of main function.
```

Lesson 29.8 Summary

An enumerated data type (enum) is a programmer defined data type. The programmer defines a new data type and set the allowable values for that data type. The compiler assigns an integer value, beginning with zero to each enumerator (value).

Enumerated data types can be used in expressions, used in a switch statement, and in comparisons.

Comparisons can be done using relational operators. Since enumerators are stored as integers an enumerator can be compared to an integer. However, we cannot set enumerators to an integer value.

End of Lesson Quiz

An _____ data type is a programmer defined data type.

You create an enumerated data type using the keyword _____.

Enumerators are stored in memory as _____.

Lesson 30
C Strings

Objectives:

- Compare and Contrast String Literals and C-Strings
- Store a string in an array
- Manipulate the C-String
- Use library functions with C-Strings

Lesson 30.1 : Overview of C-Strings

A string is any consecutive sequence of zero or more characters. A word, a sentence, a name or any sequence of characters. A string can consist of numbers, letters or special characters including spaces. In C++ strings can be represented in two different ways, a String Literal or a C-String. A string with zero characters is called a NULL string.

A String Literal (String Constant) is a literal representation of a string in a program, enclosed in double quotation marks. An example of a string literal is:

```
cout << "Welcome Back!"
```

A C-String is a sequence of characters stored in consecutive memory locations terminated by a null character or null terminator. The null character is the slash zero (\0) also referred to as ASCII code 0. An example of a C-String is:

0	1	2	3	4	5	6	7	8	9	10	11	12	13	14	15	16	17	18	19
J	o	n	D	o	e	9	8	@	u	r	l	.	c	o	m	\0			

In this example we have an array that can hold 19 characters plus the null terminator. The character string is an email address, JonDoe98@url.com. This only requires 16 elements of the array and the null terminator is found in the 17th element.

As noted in the lessons on arrays, the C String is an array of char data type and therefore is zero based. The first char position of the array is element 0. So, when calculating the number of characters in the array, don't forget to start at zero.

Lesson 30.2: Strings Stored in Arrays

Non literal strings may be stored in arrays of characters as C-Strings. These arrays of characters may be changed, compared or manipulated in a running program.

If the programmer wished to store an email address, it would first be necessary to declare an array of characters as follows:

```
char email[20];
```

This creates an array of 20 characters which would store an email address of a maximum of 19 characters. Remember, you must leave the 20th character to store the null terminator.

We can initialize this array from the program, or from the keyboard. Some other ways to create arrays to store C-Strings and initialize them are:

```
char email[] = "JonDoe98@url.com";
```

This method uses a string to initialize the array named email;

```
        char email[] = {'J', 'o', 'n', ' ', 'D ', 'o', 'e', '9', '8', '@', 'u', 'r',
'l', '.', 'c', 'o', 'm' '\0'};
```

This method initializes the array named email one character at a time. Note also included the null character at the end.

To initialize the C-String array from the program we could use one of the following coding methods:

```
char email[20];
cin >> email;

char email[20];
cin.getline(email, 20);

char email[20];
for (x=0; x<20; x++)
        {
        cin >> email;
        }
```

The first two methods allow the user to enter a string of characters to initialize the array. The first one will not allow spaces, the second one allows spaces. Since an email address cannot contain a space, either one will work for our example. The last method initializes the array using a for loop to allow the user to enter one character at a time.

Lesson 30.3 – Using library functions with C-Strings

Once a string has been stored in an array, it may be accessed and manipulated just like any other array in C++.

We will discuss three of the most common library functions used to manipulate C-Strings: strlen; strcpy; and strcmp. These require the include directive:

```
#include <cstring>
```

strlen()

The library function strlen returns the length of the string stored in the array. The contents of the array may be less than the size of the array and it may be necessary to know the exact length of the string in our program. This function returns a value we will need to provide a storage location for the returned value. The syntax for this function:

```
integervariable = strlen(arrayvariablename);

int length;
char email[20];
length = strlen(email);
```

strcpy()

The library function strcpy will copy the contents of one C-String array to a second C-String array.

```
char email[20];
char email2[20];
strcpy(email, email2);
```

This code will result in the contents of email2 being copied into email. At the end of this instruction, email will contain the original contents of email2 and email2 will remain unchanged.

strcmp()

The library function strcmp, compares the contents of one string to the contents of a second string. The comparison is done left to right, one character at a time.

```
int result = 0;
char email[20];
char email2[20];
result = strcmp(email, email2);
```

This code compares the contents of the array email to the contents of the array email2. After the comparison is done, the function returns an integer value to the calling program, which, in our example, we have stored in the variable named result. If the two arrays are equal result will contain a zero. If email2 is greater than email result will contain a negative number. If email2 is less than email, result will contain a positive number greater than 0.

Lesson 30.4 – Reading and Writing Strings

First we declare an array of type char that can hold 49 characters plus the null character and we will call this array *movieName*.

```
char movieName[50];
```

Now we put some data (a movie name) into this array. We look back to prior lessons on strings and to review the use of strings. When using the cin statement to accept strings, the first whitespace will terminate the move of characters to the variable. So if our movie name has a space in it, the variable will not contain the correct information. To solve this we use the getline() function of the cin statement. So, here is how we will get information into our array of characters.

```
cin.getline(movieName, 50);
```

Our user inputs the following string: Star Wars II Attack of the Clones

At the end of this operation the character array movieName contains the string "Star Wars II Attack of the Clones". The string is 33 characters long plus the null character, all fit within the fifty character constraint. If the movie name had been in excess of 49 characters, the overage would have been truncated.

Now that we have put some information in the array, we need to use that data. Since it is a string we might need to display the value on the screen. To do this we will use the cout statement.

```
cout << movieName;
```

The insertion operator (<<) continues to output until it encounters a null character, so the contents of our array called movieName will be displayed, in its entirety, on the screen.

Now we put this all together in a small program:

```
#include <iostream>
using namespace std;
int main()
{
        char bigstring[256];

        cout << "Enter a big string (up to 255 characters): " << endl;
        cin.getline(bigstring, 256);
        cout << "The string you entered: " << bigstring << endl;
        cout << "Your string was " << strlen(bigstring) << " characters. ";
        cout << endl;
        return 0;
}   // end of main function
```

Our example program will ask the user to enter a string of up to 255 characters. If the user enters more than that, the overage will be truncated. The string entered (up to the first 255 characters) will be displayed. Then the program uses the strlen() function to inform the user how many characters were stored in the array and output. Would this number ever be larger than 255?

Lesson 30.5 – Example Program

A program using c-strings is shown below. The application uses first names, last names and then combining the two into a full name. Then uses the functions we discussed in Lesson 30.3. The program compares the first name entered to the name "James" giving a different message if the compare is true or false. Next, the program tells the user how many characters in their first name. Then the program builds a full name out of the first name entered and the last name entered seperating them with a space. Then finishes by displaying the full name generated.

```
// cstring.cpp
// Date:
// Author:

#include <iostream>
#include <cstring>
using namespace std;
int main()
{
        char firstName[50];
        char lastName[50];
        char fullName[100];

        cout << "Enter your first name: ";
        cin.getline(firstName, 50);
        // compare strings with strcmp()
        if (strcmp(firstName, "James") == 0)
             cout << "We share the same first name!" << endl;
        else
             cout << "We have different first names!" << endl;
        // show the length of the string entered using strlen()
        cout << "Your first name is: " << strlen(firstName) << " letters long."
<< endl;
```

```
        cout << "Enter your last name: ";
        cin.getline(lastName, 50);

        fullName[0] = '\0';                    // sets the first char to null char.
        strcat(fullName, firstName); // input the first name
        strcat(fullName, " ");        // input a blank to sep names
        strcat(fullName, lastName);        // input the last name
        cout << "Your complete name is: " << fullName << endl;

        return 0;
} // end of main function
```

Lesson 30.6 – Summary

Before the ANSI/ISO C++ standard of 1998 the C++ programming language did not have a data type for strings of data. Prior to this C++ had inherited the same technique for storing and using strings used by the C language. C stored strings of characters in a character array. The programmer had to set up an array of data type char, large enough to store the string plus one more character to store the null character that signified the end of the string. If the programmer did not allow sufficient space for a string, it was truncated.

C-Strings can be input using the getline function and displayed using the cout statement. The include directive cstring contains several functions for using arrays of characters (C-Strings). The strlen() can be used to determine the length of a string, strcpy() to copy a string, and strcmp() to compare two strings.

End of Lesson Quiz

A _____ is any consecutive sequence of zero or more characters.

A string with zero characters is referred to as a _____ string.

The _____ _____ is an array of char data type.

Lesson 31
Structured Data (structs)

Objectives:

- Explain abstract data types
- Access structure members
- Initialize a structure
- Declare and use arrays of structures
- Use structures in functions.

Lesson 31.1 Abstract Data Types

An Abstract Data Type (ADT) is a key concept to object oriented programming and computer programming in general. C++ has a mechanism for creating abstract data types called structs.

In previous lessons, data types were defined as several "primitive data types". They are basic parts of the C++ programming language. The data type defines what kind of data can be stored in a variable. It also defines the various arithmetic and relational operators that can be used with data of that type.

An ADT is a data type created by the programmer, which is composed of one or more primitive data types. The programmer controls the acceptable values for the data type and the operations that may be performed on this data type.

Lesson 31.2 Define Structures

Up to this point, all programs have kept data in individual variables or arrays of individual variables. Arrays limited the programmer to groups of data of the same data type. Structs allow the programmer to group data where a relationship exists between data of different data types.

In Lesson 24 we discussed File Input and File Output. Files are composed of a sequence of records and each record is composed of related fields of data. If we were writing a file containing information about the employees in our company it might look like this:

```
RECORD 1     employee number
             employee last name
             employee first name
             employee payRate
RECORD 2     employee number
             employee last name
             employee first name
             employee payRate
RECORD 3     employee number
             employee last name
             employee first name
             employee payRate
RECORD 4     employee number
             employee last name
             employee first name
             employee payRate
```

The data we would like to track for each employee is their employee number, employee last name, employee first name, and their rate of pay. The declared variables to store this data may look something like this:

```
int employeenbr;
string lastname;
string firstname;
float payRate;
```

Note there are three different types of data we need to store. The ability to handle the different types of data is the real power of the struct, building a new datatype from several primitive types.

Each record read from or written to the file would require that we transfer each of the four fields individually. Not a big problem for a small record like this but could be a bigger challenge when writing larger, more complex record structures found in many "real world" applications.

The solution in C++ is to use a struct. Creating a struct that reflects the fields within a record can make the data input and output files more manageable. The syntax for creating a struct is:

```
SYNTAX:
    struct structurename
    {
        datatype field1;
        datatype field2;
        datatype field3;
             .
        datatype fieldn;
    };
```

The syntax consists of the keyword, struct followed by the name assigned to the structure (this becomes a new data type), and must conform to the naming convention for any variable. Then within a set of "curly braces", the data type and field name for each field in the structure, in the order they will be read or written. These, unlike variables, may not be initialized to a value.

The first step is to go over how to create a struct within a program. The code to declare a struct for employee data is as follows:

```
    struct employeeinfo
    {
        int employeenbr;
        string lastname;
        string firstname;
        float payRate;
    };
```

The structure must be defined before the main function. Then used in the main function (or any other function) by declaring a new variable of that new data type. In our example above, the data type is employeeinfo.

When we need a variable of the datatype employeeinfo, we declare the variable as follows:

```
    employeeinfo employee2009;
```

This creates a variable that can store an integer value for employeenbr; a string value for lastname; a string value for firstname and a float value for tuition. These are called members. The variable name employee2009 contains four members (employeenbr, lastname, firstname, tuition).

Lesson 31.3 Access Structure Members

When we accessed a cell in an array we used the array name and the index number of the cell containing the data we needed. Accessing data in a struct is quite different. There is no index number. In place of that we use the name of the structure, the dot operator and the member name. The syntax is:

```
SYNTAX:
        structvariablename.membername
```

When we want to access the employee's last name in the struct we are using, the information is accessed as:

```
employee2009.lastname
```

This will allow access to the member called lastname in the current record. We can then put data in the member several different ways.

```
cin >> employee2009.lastname;

employee2009.lastname = "Smith";
```

We can also move data from one structure variable to another structure variable of the same type. To illustrate this we will create a second structure to hold archived employee data.

```
struct employee2009
{
        int employeenbr;
        string lastname;
        string firstname;
        float payRate;
};
struct employeeArchive
{
        int employeenbr;
        string lastname;
        string firstname;
        float payRate;
};
```

Another way to create an identical structure is:

```
struct employee2009
{
        int employeenbr;
        string lastname;
        string firstname;
        float payRate;
};
employee2009.employeeArchive
```

We now have two identical structures, one called employee2009 and the other called employeeArchive. Both structures are of the same data type, employeeinfo. Moving data between the two structures is done as follows:

```
employeeArchive.employeenbr = employee2009.employeenbr;
```

This command copies the contents of the member of the employee2009 structure to the corresponding member of the employeeArchive structure.

Lesson 31.4 Comparison and Structures

Comparisons of structures must be done member by member. There is no aggregate comparison for the struct, just like we discussed in arrays. So, the bottom line is you must compare each member individually.

If you simply compared our two structs, it would not work. The following instruction is an illegal command. There is NO aggregate comparison allowed.

```
If (employee2009 == employeeArchive)
    {
    True Statements;
    }
```

Again using our two arrays employee2009 and employeeArchive, let us compare to see if we have a name match in both arrays. The expression in an decision structure would look something like this:

```
if (employee2009.lastname == employeeArchive.lastname &&
    employee2009.firstname == employeeArchive.firstname)
        True Statements
```

This compares the member named lastname of employee2008 with the member named lastname of employeeArchive.

Lesson 31.5 Declare Arrays in Structures

You can use an array as a member of a structure. Our example for this lesson is to build a struct containing an array and an integer variable that will contain the length of the array (how many items are in the array). The struct looks like this:

```
struct rainfall
{
    double weekly[52];
    int lendata;
};
```

To get data into and out of a struct that uses an array you would need code that is similar to this:

```
rainfall annualRain;
int week;
annualRain.lendata = 0;

for (week = 0; week < 52; week++)
    {
        cout << "Enter rainfall for week " << week + 1 << ":   ";
        cin >> annualRain.weekly[week];
        lendata++;
    }
```

This for loop asks the user for a weekly rainfall amount, stores it in the appropriate element of the array, and finally keeping count of how many items in the array by incrementing the member for that purpose.

Lesson 31.6 Use Arrays in Structures

Now that there is data in the array how can we use this information. Continuing with the example in the last lesson, let's code a for loop to print out the weekly amounts and then at the end print the average rainfall.

```
double sumRainfall = 0.0;

for (week = 0; week <= lendata -1; week++)
      {
              sumRainfall = annualRain.weekly[week];
              cout << "Week " << lendata << "is "
                   << annualRain.weekly[week] << " inches." << endl;
      }
   cout << "The total rainfall for " << lendata << " weeks. "
          << sumRainfall << " inches."
   cout <<  "The average rainfall is " << sumRainfall / lendata << " inches. "
<< endl;
```

Lesson 31.7 Use Arrays of Structs

Suppose we wanted to track the rainfall and temperature for 10 major cities? How do we incorporate our rainfall struct into an array? The definition of the struct rainfall is as follows:

```
struct rainfall
{
      double weekly;
      double temp;
};
```

Now using the rainfall data type we declare an array named cityrain with 10 elements.

```
rainfall cityrain[10]
```

Now, let's create a for loop to put data into our array:

```
int counter;
for (counter = 0; counter < 50; counter++)
{
      cout << "Enter rainfall for city " << counter << ": ";
      cin >> rainfall[counter].weekly;
      cout << "Enter the temperature: ";
      cin >> rainfall[counter].temp;
}
```

Then we write the code to sum the rainfall for all ten cities and get an average.

```
double sumrainfall = 0.0;
double sumtemp = 0.0;
for (counter = 0; counter < 50; counter++)
{
      sumrainfall = rainfall[counter].weekly;
```

```
            sumtemp = rainfall[counter].temp;
    }

        cout << "Average Rainfall for 10 cities: " << sumrainfall / 10 << endl;
        cout << "Average Tempearture for 10 cities: " << sumtemp / 10 << endl;
```

The loop sums the rainfall and temperatures and when complete, calculates the average rainfall and the average temperature for the ten cities.

Lesson 31.8 Use Structs with Functions.

Functions are one of the most valuable tools in C++ programming, yet one of the most dreaded by those learning the language. Passing arguments to a function and passing results back is often the biggest problem. This lesson will demonstrate how to pass a struct to a function and get information back to the calling program.

Structure variables may be passed as arguments to a function. Like other variables, members of a struct may be passed as function arguments. Example of a struct containing the elements to calculate simple interest:

```
    // A struct named interest
    struct interest
    {
        double principal;
        double rate;
        double term;
        double amt;
    }

    // Declare a variable of type interest named payment
    interest payment;

    // function call to return the interest calculation to the amt member
    payment.amt = calc(payment.principal, payment.rate, payment.term);

    // A function that multiplies three numbers of type double
    double calc(double x, double y, double z)
    {
        return x * y * z;
    }
```

This example has a struct that contains the amounts required to calculate simple interest as well as the calculated amount. The program declares a variable of type interest named payment. The function is a generic function that accepts 3 arguments of type double and returns the value of the three arguments multiplied by each other.

The function call passes the principal, the rate and the term to the function which returns the value to be stored in the member of the function assigned to hold the amount (amt).

Lesson 31.9 Sample Program

A simple program to calculate the area and perimeter of a rectangle using the struct and function capabilities.

```cpp
// structprog.cpp
// Date:
// Author:
// This program uses a function that returns a structure.
#include <iostream>
#include <cmath>
#include <iomanip>
using namespace std;

struct rectangle
{
    double length;
    double width;
    double area;
    double perimeter;
};

// prototype for function getdata
rectangle getdata();

int main()
{
    // Define Variables
    rectangle rec1;
    // Get Data
    rec1 = getdata();
    // Calculate
    rec1.area = rec1.length * rec1.width;
    rec1.perimeter = (rec1.width * 2) + (rec1.length * 2);

    // Display Results
    cout << fixed << showpoint;
    cout << setprecision(3);

    cout << "The area of the rectangle is: " << setw(8);
    cout << rec1.area << endl;
    cout << "The perimeter of the rectangle is: << setw(6)
        << rec1.perimeter << endl;
    return 0;
}   // end of main function

rectangle getdata()
{
    rectangle funrec;
    cout << "Enter the length of the rectangle: ";
    cin >> funrec.length;
    cout << "Enter the width of the rectangle: ";
    cin >> funrec.width;
    return funrec;
}   // end of getdata function
```

Lesson 31.10 Summary

Up to this point we have only worked with primitive data types. Structured Data (structs) are Abstract Data Types (ADT) which is a new data type comprised of several primitive data types. These new data types have the ability to handle several different data types and that is the power of the ADTs. Each primitive data type within a struct is called a member. To access a primitive within a struct we use the structure name, the dot operator, and the member name.

Comparison of structures must be done member by member. An array can be a member of a structure, and you can create arrays of structures.

Functions are a valuable programming tool in C++ and important to good programming structure. Structs can be passed as arguments to functions. The calling program must pass arguments in the form (structure name, dot operator, and member name). Note, you do not pass the entire structure, only the members required by the function.

End of Lesson Quiz

C++ has a mechanism for creating abstract data types called _____.

An _____ _____ _____ is a data type created by the programmer, composed of one or more primitive data types.

Comparison of structures must be done _____ _____ _____.

Lesson 32
An Introduction to Pointers

Objectives:

- Obtain the address of a variable.
- Declare a pointer variable
- Use pointers in arithmetic.
- Initialize a pointer
- Compare Pointers
- Use a pointer as a function parameter.

Lesson 32.1 Review of variables

In a prior lesson, variables were discussed and defined as storage areas inside a program to hold pieces of data. Variables have names because using numeric addresses would make programming difficult. However, this is a human limitation because the computer works only with the actual addresses. So, the C++ language has a provision for working with variables that use the address of a variable.

When a variable is declared, the amount of memory required to hold the specific data type is reserved. The operating system assigns the location in memory at runtime. There may be instances when it is necessary to know the exact location where the operating system has stored the contents of a variable.

Lesson 32.2 Address of Operator

The address that is used to locate a variable and its contents within memory is called a reference to that variable. This reference to a variable can be obtained by putting an ampersand sign (&) in front of the variable identifier. The ampersand sign is called the reference operator, or called the "address of" operator.

```
a = &b;
```

This instruction will store the address of the variable b into the memory location for variable a. It will not store the contents of b only the address of the contents of b.

```
b = 12;          address 2121
c = b;           address 2122
d = &b;          address 2123
```

If the variable b was stored in memory location 2121, variable c stored in memory location 2122, and d stored in memory location 2123. At the end of the execution of the above code, b would still hold the value 12. The variable c would also contain the value 12 as the contents of b were copied to c in the second instruction. Look at the third instruction, because of the ampersand in front of the b in the rightmost operand, the address of the variable b is stored in the variable d. So, the contents of the variable d points to the contents of the variable b which is 12.

Lesson 32.3 Pointers

A variable that stores a reference to another variable is called a pointer. With a pointer the program can directly access the contents of another variable. To do this the pointer's identifier is preceded by an asterisk (*). The asterisk is translated as "value pointed by". The value of a pointer variable is an address. When you declare a variable the data type is the data type stored at the memory location it points to. The syntax of a pointer declaration:

```
datatype  *identifier;
```

Example:

```
int *a;
char *b;
```

In our example the variable named a stores the address of a memory location that contains an integer. The variable named b stores the address of a memory location that contains a character.

There is often some confusion on how pointers are written with the placement of the asterisk. Let's look at three examples:

```
int    *x;
int    *   x;
int*   x;
```

What is the difference? The answer is, there is no difference. Where the asterisk appears between the data type and the identifier, makes no difference.

In the statement:

```
int *x, y;
```

Only the variable x is a pointer, the variable y is an integer variable. It could also be written as:

```
int* x, y;
```

As you can see this may be misleading. So, to avoid confusion the asterisk should always be attached to the identifier. If the statement was written as:

```
int *x, *y;
```

Both identifiers x and y would be pointer variables.

Lesson 32.4 Using Pointers and Address of Operators

Now, let's look at how we would use these new concepts in a program. First, a simple little program to illustrate these concepts.

```
#include <iostream>
using namespace std;
int main()
{
      int num1 = 88;
      int *ref1;
      ref1 = &num1;
      cout << *ref1 << endl;
      *ref1 = 99;
      cout << num1 << endl;
      return 0;
}   // end of main function
```

The result of running this program is that the contents of the variable num1 (88) will be printed

out by the first output statement. At this point *ref1 points at the contents of the variable num1.
Then the program changes the memory contents pointed to by *ref1 to a new value 99. The last
output statement will then print out the new contents of num1 which is 88.

One use of pointers and address of operators is in addressing arrays. Here is a sample program
that uses these new concepts to address the contents of an array and print them to the common
output.

```
#include <iostream>
#include <iomanip>
using namespace std;
int main()
{
        double rain[5] = {0.01, 0.8, 1.1, 0.02, 0.0};
        double *rainptr;
        int x;

        rainptr = rain;
        cout << setprecision(2);
        cout << fixed << showpoint;
        cout << "The 5 days of rainfall array" << endl;
        for (x=0; x<5; x++)
        {
                cout << rainptr(x) << " ";
        }
        cout << endl << endl << endl;
        cout << "Or a different approach" << endl;
        for (x=0; x<5; x++)
        {
                cout << *(rain + x) << " ";
        }
        cout << endl;
        return 0;
} // end of main function
```

The output of this program should look like this:

```
The 5 days of rainfall array
0.01 0.8 1.1 0.02 0.0
Or a different approach
0.01 0.8 1.1 0.02 0.0
```

A point of interest is that after the pointer variable rainptr was declared using the asterisk, it was
not necessary to use the asterisk in the other code statements. However, the argument for using
the asterisk in every instance is to show that that variable references a memory address. This
may help in debugging the program in the future.

Lesson 32.5 Sample Program

A simple program to demonstrate using an array and pointers.

```
// Program using an array and pointers
// Date:
// Author:

#include <iostream>
#include <iomanip>
```

```cpp
using namespace std;
int main()
{
        float regionSales[4] =
                {10000.01, 9345.87, 12873.15, 8450.02};
        float *rsalesptr;
        int x;

        rsalesptr = regionSales;
        cout << fixed << showpoint;
        cout << setprecision(2);
        cout << "The 4 regional sales amounts array" << endl;
        for (x=0; x<4; x++)
        {
                if (x == 0)
                cout << "North Region: $" << rsalesptr[x] << endl;
                if (x == 1)
                cout << "South Region: $" << rsalesptr[x] << endl;
                if (x == 2)
                cout << "East Region:  $" << rsalesptr[x] << endl;
                if (x == 3)
                cout << "West Region:  $" << rsalesptr[x] << endl;
        }
        cout << endl;
        cout << "Or a different approach" << endl;
        cout << endl;
        for (x=0; x<4; x++)
        {
                if (x == 0)
                cout << "North Region: $" << *(regionSales + x) << endl;
                if (x == 1)
                cout << "South Region: $" << *(regionSales + x) << endl;
                if (x == 2)
                cout << "East Region:  $" << *(regionSales + x) << endl;
                if (x == 3)
                cout << "West Region:  $" << *(regionSales + x) << endl;

        }
        cout << endl;
        return 0;
} // end of main function
```

Lesson 32.6 Summary

Pointers are a useful part of efficient C++ programming. In simple terms a pointer is a variable that holds the memory address of another variable. Pointer variables are declared the same way other variables are declared but prefixed by a "*". The pointers data type must match the data type of the variable it points to.

End of Lesson Quiz

An ampersand (&) in front of a variable identifier is called the _____ _____.

A variable that stores a reference to another variable is called a _____.

A pointer's identifier is preceded by an _____.

Start Programming with C++

Appendix A
End of Lesson Quiz Answers

Section I

Lesson 1
  Source File
  Analysis
  Readability

Lesson 2
  Word Problem
  Flowcharting
  Pseudocode
  Input Processing Output

Lesson 3
  Variable
  Main
  Word Problems

Lesson 4
  Test Data
  Demonstrate ability to use spreadsheets.
  Changed

Section II

Lesson 5
  Letter
  Camel Case
  Double, Float

Lesson 6
  Constants
  Comments
  %
  =
  Parentheses

Lesson 7
  Common OUTput
  <<
  fixed
  setw()

Lesson 24
    Field
    Sequential
    ifstream

Section VII

Lesson 25
    Arrays
    Subscript
    0

Lesson 26
    Parallel Arrays
    Data Type
    different

Lesson 27
    Spreadsheet
    Row, Column
    same

Lesson 28
    Pointer
    Prototype, Header
    Reuse Code

Section VII

Lesson 29
    Enumerated
    enumerated
    Integer

Lesson 30
    String
    NULL
    C String

Lesson 31
    Structs
    Abstract Data Type
    member by member

Lesson 32
    Reference Operator
    Pointer
    Asterisk

Start Programming with C++

Appendix B
How to Compile a C++ Program

Welcome Program
Using Visual C++.NET 2010

These instructions are for those using Visual C++.NET 2010. If you do not follow these instructions EXACTLY you may experience problems. I suggest you place a folder in the root directory of you C: drive named "data". This will simplify finding your project files.

NOTE: When you finish a project you should exit Visual Studio.NET completely before starting the next project.

To Use Visual C++.NET 2010

1. On the Start Page Check the My Profile Tab to make sure you are a C++ user. Other classes use other programming languages so it may not be set exactly as you left the PC.
2. On the Start page under the project tab click on NEW PROJECT
Alternative is File > New > New Project

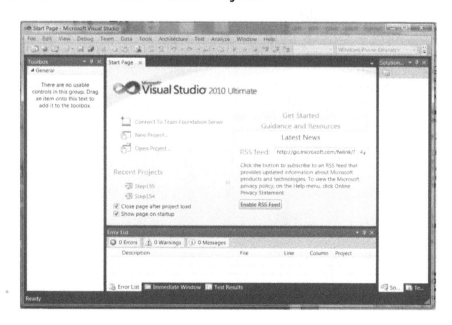

3. On the New Project Dialog box
Project Type = Visual C++ Project
Templates = Win32 Console Project (Icon)
Name = (The name you have selected for your program) this one is
welcome
Location = C:\data
Click on OK

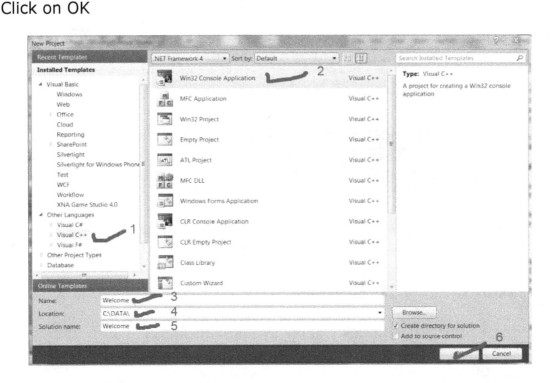

4. Win32 Application Wizard will open
5. Click on APPLICATION SETTINGS
Application Type = Console Application
Additional options = Check EMPTY PROJECT
Add support for = All boxes unchecked
6. Click on FINISH

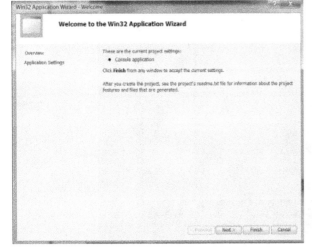

7. In Solution Explorer Window right click on folder marked SOURCE FILES

From pop-up menu select ADD
From pop-up menu select Add New Item.
In Add New Item Dialog Box

Categories = Visual C++
Templates = C++ File(.cpp) icon
Name = (The name you have selected for your program) this one is **welcome**
Location = C:\data\your project name (you should not have to change this setting)
Click on OPEN

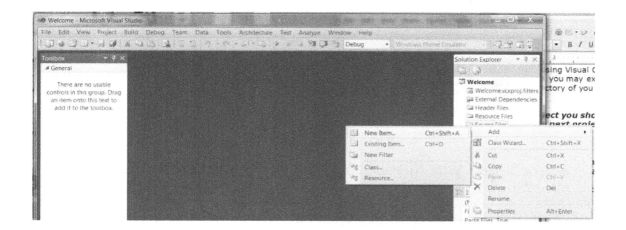

This results in this dialog box.

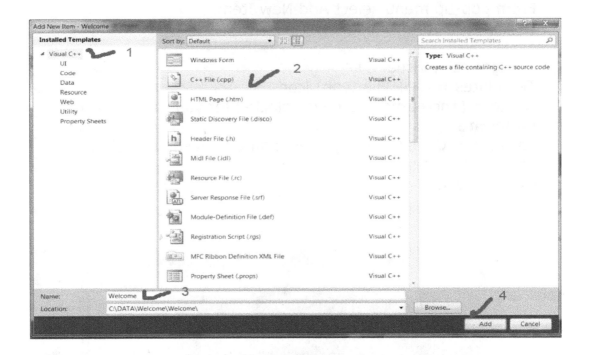

8. Now you can type in your source code for your program:

```
// Welcome.cpp
// Date:          (put today's date here)
// Author:        (put your name here)

#include<iostream>
using namespace std;

int main()
{
     cout << "Welcome to the C++ Workshop" << endl;
     return 0;
}    // End of Main Function
```

9. When finished go to the menu and click on DEBUG

Click on the START DEBUGGING selection
Note: you may get a warning message that tells you your project data is out of date. Would you like to build them? ANSWER = YES

10. If Successful click on the menu item DEBUG
    Click on the selection START WITHOUT DEBUGGING to see your results.

If not successful, find and fix your errors and return to step 9

Your data files, (if you followed my directions) will be in the folder :
        C:\data\yourprojectname (welcome)
For the source file (.cpp) it will be in the folder:
        C:\data\yourprojectname (welcome)
For the executable module (.exe) it will be in the folder:
        C:\data\yourprojectname\debug
The welcome.cpp and welcome.exe files may be used on another computer.

DevTest Program
Using DevC++

These instructions are for those using DevC++ from bloodshed.net. If you do not follow these instructions EXACTLY you may experience problems. You can obtain DevC++ as a free download from the web site www.bloodshed.net.

> ***NOTE: When you finish a project you should exit DevC++ completely before starting the next project.***

To Use DevC++ Version 4.9.9.2

When you start DevC++ you will see a screen like this. I find the "Tip of the Day" an interesting read and sometimes some good programming tips.

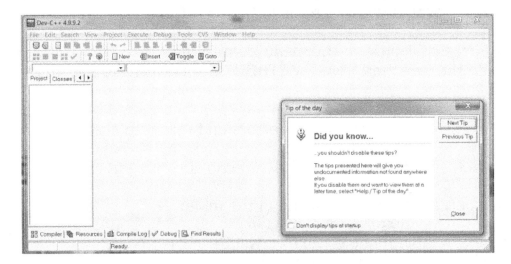

To begin your new program, click on the "***File***" menu item, select "***New***", and then select "***Project***" to reserve a file area named with your project name.

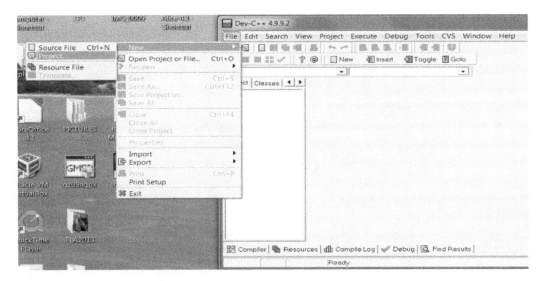

Once a new Project is selected a "**New Project**" dialog box will appear. Here you
need to select the "**Console Application**" icon under the "**Basic**" tab, and enter your
project name in the text box under the title "**Name**". Make sure the "**C++ Project**"
radio button is selected. When this is complete, click on the "**OK**" button.

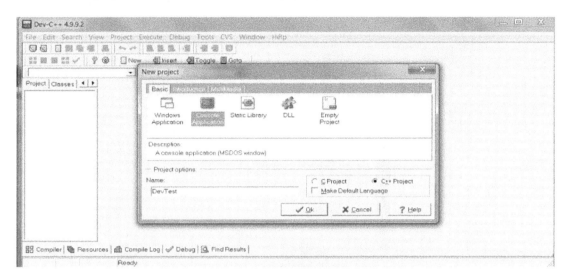

We are now presented with a screen containing a template for a C++ program. Yes,
DevC++ gives a basic template for most C++ programs. You will see some
differences from what I have presented in the book but you need not change them as
they will not affect the compiling or processing of the program. The obvious
differences are:

- **#include<stdlib>** This includes the standard library. This is necessary in
  some systems for the "system" command.
- **system("PAUSE");** This stops the program so the user can read the screen
  before the program exits.
- **int main(int argc, char *argv[1])** The arguments need not be changed.
- **return EXIT_SUCCESS;** return statement using a system variable

These differences can be left alone, they will not affect the outcome of the program.

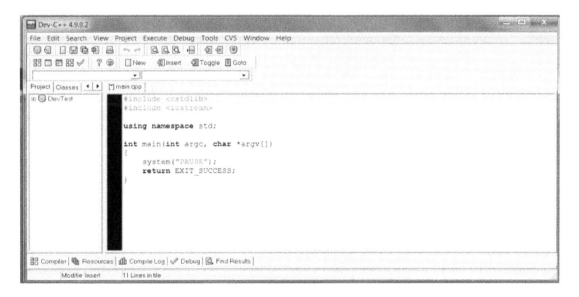

Now we are ready to enter the program code in the main function. Once the code has been entered, the "Compilation" process can begin. To Compile a program in the DevC++ compiler, go back to the top menu and select the "**Execute**" menu. Then select the "**Compile**" choice (or enter Ctrl + F9 from the keyboard) to compile the program.

If your compilation process has NO SYNTAX ERRORS, you will have a project folder with an executable file (.exe file) in the project folder. If an error did occur you will see a screen with a list of errors at the bottom (see ERROR SCREEN at the end of this appendix). You must fix these errors and recompile. A new executable file will not be produced if there are any SYNTAX errors.

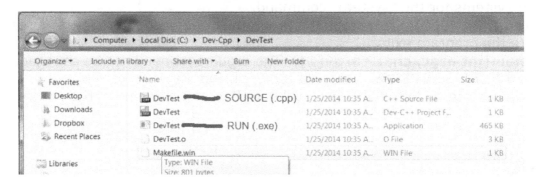

To Save your file, the save choices are under the "**File**" menu. The "**Save in:**" text box should display the name of your "Project" folder. In the "**File name**" text box, enter the name you would like to give your executable file. Once you have made these changes, click on the "**Save**" button.

Now we are ready to run the application. To run your application, select the "**Execute**" choice from the menu and then select the "**Run**" choice.

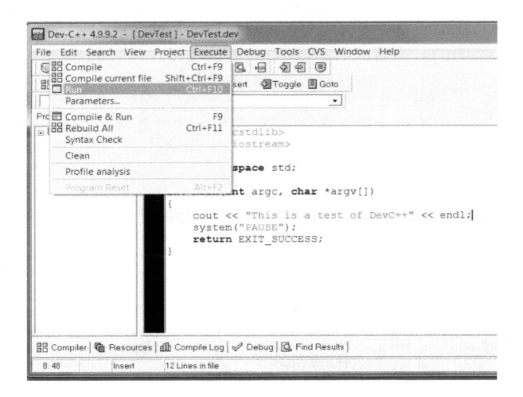

Running our DevTest application will result in the screen below.

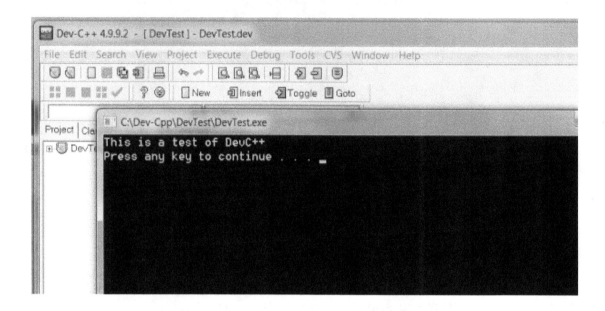

Another way to run our new application is to go to the Project folder and Double Click on the Application file (.exe file). In the figure below you will see the contents of our DevTest Project file. The Source (.cpp file) and the Executable (.exe file) files are marked.

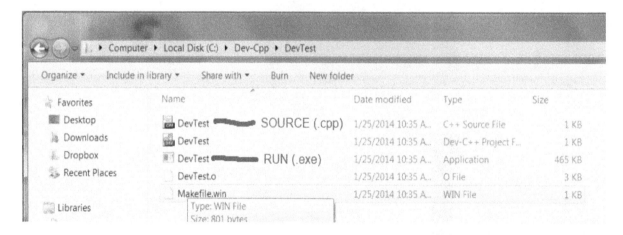

As we examine the Project folder we find the Source File (.cpp file) and the Executable File (.exe file). We also see a file of the type "DevC++ Project File. If we Double Click on this file and you are placed back in the DevC++ development environment. A great way to restart your work on the project.

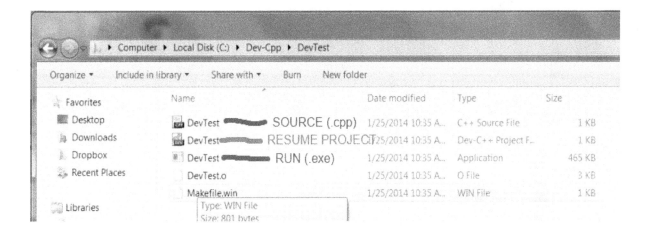

You will have to click on the .cpp file in the left panel to show the code.

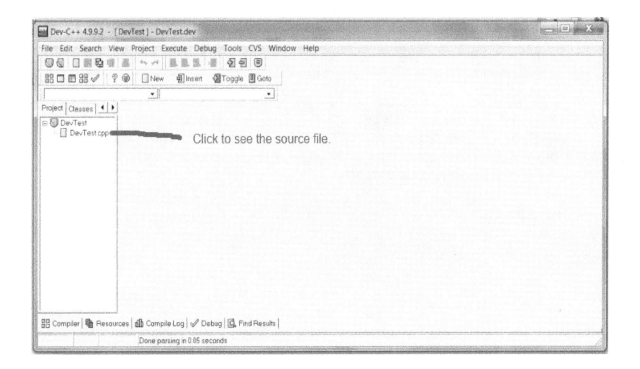

ERROR SCREEN:

Below is an example of a compilation that encountered a SYNTAX error.

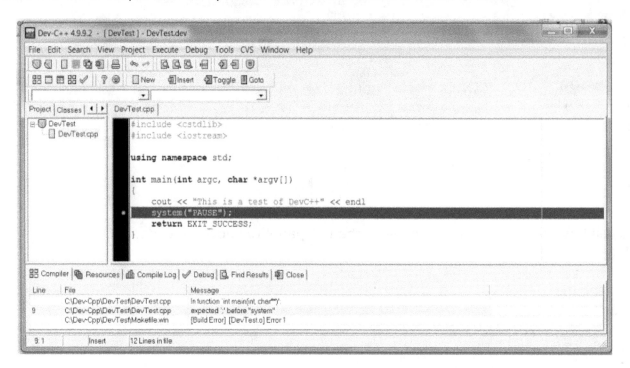

Note the highlighted code line, this shows the "*approximate*" location of the error.
This may, or may not, be the line in error. In this case it is the line after the error. In
the bottom panel the error is "***expected ";" before system***". In this case we
neglected to put a semi-colon after the "*endl*" statement on the previous line. Make
this fix, recompile and all should be correct.

C++ Program
Using g++ in Linux

These instructions are for those using the g++ compiler on a Linux system. If you do not follow these instructions EXACTLY you may experience problems. You will need to have a current Linux Distribution as well as the g++ compiler installed.

NOTE: When you finish a project you should exit g++ completely before starting the next project.

To Use g++

Create your C++ source code in a text editor. In this example I used the Kate text editor. My Linux distribution is Ubuntu 12.10. The source code file name is **LinuxTest.cpp**.

The first command "ls" shows the files in the current directory. Since the source file created is in the Documents Folder, the second command changes the current directory to the "**Documents**" directory. The third command lists the contents of the Documents directory where we find the ***LinuxTest.cpp*** source program.

```
jim@jim-Inspiron-6000: ~/Documents
jim@jim-Inspiron-6000:~/Documents$ g++ LinuxTest.cpp
jim@jim-Inspiron-6000:~/Documents$ ls -l
total 40
-rwxrwxr-x 1 jim jim 7896 Jan 26 12:26 a.out
-rw-rw-r-- 1 jim jim  125 Jan 26 12:17 LinuxTest.cpp
-rw-rw-r-- 1 jim jim  144 Jan 26 12:17 LinuxTest.cpp~
-rw-rw-r-- 1 jim jim  166 Jan 19 13:28 twonum.py
-rw-rw-r-- 1 jim jim  144 Jan 19 13:30 voteone.py
-rw-rw-r-- 1 jim jim  285 Jan 19 13:46 votetwo.py
-rw-rw-r-- 1 jim jim  287 Jan 19 13:46 votetwo.py~
-rw-rw-r-- 1 jim jim  174 Jan 19 13:49 wkrain.py
-rw-rw-r-- 1 jim jim  174 Jan 19 13:49 wkrain.py~
jim@jim-Inspiron-6000:~/Documents$ ./a.out
Hello, Linux World!
jim@jim-Inspiron-6000:~/Documents$
```

The next command "$ g++ LinuxTest.cpp" compiles the source code but since there was no output file indicated the default name "**a.out**" is used. We confirm this with the ls -l command. Then to execute the program use the command:

```
$ ./a.out
```

The a.out program is executed and you can see the message on the screen.

```
jim@jim-Inspiron-6000: ~/Documents
jim@jim-Inspiron-6000:~/Documents$ g++ -Wall -W -Werror LinuxTest.cpp -o test
jim@jim-Inspiron-6000:~/Documents$ ls -l
total 20
-rwxrwxr-x 1 jim jim 7896 Jan 26 12:26 a.out
-rw-rw-r-- 1 jim jim  125 Jan 26 12:17 LinuxTest.cpp
-rwxrwxr-x 1 jim jim 7896 Jan 26 12:31 test
jim@jim-Inspiron-6000:~/Documents$ chmod +x test
jim@jim-Inspiron-6000:~/Documents$ ls -l
total 20
-rwxrwxr-x 1 jim jim 7896 Jan 26 12:26 a.out
-rw-rw-r-- 1 jim jim  125 Jan 26 12:17 LinuxTest.cpp
-rwxrwxr-x 1 jim jim 7896 Jan 26 12:31 test
jim@jim-Inspiron-6000:~/Documents$ ./test
Hello, Linux World!
jim@jim-Inspiron-6000:~/Documents$
```

The next compile command places the output in a file named "test". The command:

```
$ g++ -Wall -W -Werror LinuxTest.cpp -o test
```

This command compiles the program and places the output in a file named "test"

We use the "ls -l" command to verify the creation of the file. Note that in this version of the compiler, the file is executable "-rwxrwxr-x" is the file's permissions. This is not true of all versions. Therefore use the command:

```
$ chmod +x test
```
This adds the executable permissions to the "test" file.

Then to execute the program use the command:

```
$ ./test
```

The "**test**" program is executed and you can see the message on the screen.

If you have errors:

The semi-colon is missing at the end of the cout statement. The run using the command: "**$ g++ LinuxTest.cpp**" resulted in an error message indicating the problem in the program. The command: "**$g++ -Wall -W -Werror LinuxTest.cpp -o test**" gives the same error. Not bad for one error but if there are numerous errors it can be a problem. The "**ls -l**" command shows that neither command generated an executable file.

Start Programming with C++

Appendix C
IPO Chart Material

Analysis of Restaurant: Tip IPO Chart.

Tip Calculation

Write a IPO Chart for a program that computes the tax and tip on a restaurant bill for a patron. The user will be asked to enter the cost of the meal and the amount of tip he/she wishes to leave. Display the meal cost, tax amount, tip amount and the total bill on the screen. Then, create the test data for this problem.

IPO Chart for: _____Project 4 Tip Calculation_____

INPUT	PROCESSING	OUTPUT

Inputs:
mealAmount
tipPct
taxPct = 5%
	Processing:
	
	1. Ask user for mealAmount
	2. Ask user for tipPct
	3. Calculate Tax
	   taxAmount = mealAmount * taxPct
	4. Calculate Tax
	   tipAmount = mealAmount * tipPct
	5. Calculate totalBill
	   totalBill = mealAmount + taxAmount + tipAmount
	6. Display mealCost
	7. Display taxAmount
	8. Display tipAmount
	9. Display totalBill
		Outputs:
		mealCost
		taxAmount
		tipAmount
		totalBill

Above is a proper solution for this problem. NOT THE ONLY SOLUTION but an example of a proper solution.

I prefer pseudocode (a personal preference) for my IPO chart. If you prefer using the flowchart symbols your PROCESSING column will be the flowchart but the INPUT and OUTPUT columns should look similar to mine.

This analysis and chart creation of each program will help you code a solution in less time. The time you spend doing your analysis and chart will be less that the time you will spend debugging a poorly conceived program.

First, find all the outputs required by the program. Next, you need to figure out the algorithms to provide those outputs. Then you need to list the inputs (data) needed to plug in to those algorithms. Lastly, put down the steps needed to solve those algorithms and produce all of the required outputs.

Start Programming with C++

Appendix D
C++ Keywords

This is a list of the keywords in Standard C++. These were also present in the C programming language and were carried over to the C++ programming language. They are:

C++ Reserved Words

auto	double	int	struct
break	else	long	switch
case	enum	register	typedef
char	extern	return	union
const	float	short	unsigned
continue	for	signed	void
default	goto	sizeof	volatile
do	if	static	while

There are also 30 reserved words new to C++ that did not exist in C. These words are:

asm	false	public	try
bool	friend	protected	typeid
catch	inline	reinterpret_cast	typename
class	mutable	static_cast	using
const_cast	namespace	template	virtual
delete	new	this	wchar_t
dynamic_cast	operator	throw	
explicit	private	true	

When the standard ASCII character set is used the following are not used as reserved words. However, when other character sets that do not have characters that are required for C++ programming, the words in this list provide the programmer with alternatives. It is a good idea to refrain from using these words as identifiers in your program.

and	bitor	not_eq	xor
and_eq	compl	or	xor_eq
bitand	not	or_eq	

While programming in C++ some words are encountered that are often thought of as keywords but are actually called "predefined identifiers". They are not reserved words or keywords and could be used as identifiers in a program. They can be used but it is NOT a good idea. If used within a program they could be confusing to the programmer and possibly some compilers.

Some of these predefined identifiers are:

cin	INT_MIN	main	std
cout	INT_MAX	MAX_RAND	string
endl	iomanip	npos	
include	iostream	NULL	

I have included the following program to illustrate using some of the predefined identifiers in a program as a variable name. I do not recommend using this within your programs, it just illustrates that it can be done. This program compiled without error and ran in Microsoft's Visual Studio.

```
#include<iostream>
using namespace std;

int main()
{
    int cin;
    int main;

    cin = 5;
    main = 10;

    cout << cin << " " << main << endl;
    return 0;
}       // end of main function
```

Again, this is for illustrative purposes and not recommended for use in your programs.

www.ingramcontent.com/pod-product-compliance
Lightning Source LLC
Chambersburg PA
CBHW080407060326
40689CB00019B/4164

9 781492 214441